No
Best
work!
Bob

lit

MW00592700

PRACADEMICS
(and) COMMUNITY
CHANGE

12/29/2010

Nancy,
Thanks for all that you do
to help so many individuals who
wants to learn more about
Nonprofit Management. May God
continue to bless the works of
your hands.

God Bless,

Odell

PRACADEMICS
and COMMUNITY CHANGE

A True Story of Nonprofit
Development and Social
Entrepreneurship
during Welfare Reform

Rev. Odell Cleveland and Prof. Robert Wineburg

LYCEUM
BOOKS, INC.

Published by

LYCEUM BOOKS, INC.
5758 S. Blackstone Ave.
Chicago, Illinois 60637
773+643-1903 (Fax)
773+643-1902 (Phone)
lyceum@lyceumbooks.com
http://www.lyceumbooks.com

6 5 4 3 2 1   11 12 13 14

ISBN 978-1-933478-98-2

Library of Congress Cataloging-in-Publication Data

Cleveland, Odell.
Pracademics and community change : a true story of nonprofit development and social entrepreneurship / Odell Cleveland and Robert Wineburg.
    p. cm.
Includes index.
ISBN 978-1-933478-98-2 (pbk. : alk. paper)
1. Faith-based human services--North Carolina--Greensboro. 2. Church and social problems--North Carolina--Greensboro. 3. Occupational training--North Carolina--Greensboro. 4. Poor--Services for--North Carolina--Greensboro. 5. Community development--North Carolina--Greensboro. 6. Nonprofit organizations--North Carolina--Greensboro. 7. Cleveland, Odell. 8. Wineburg, Robert J. I. Wineburg, Robert J. II. Title.
HN80.G69C54 2011
362.5'84--dc22
                                                                          2010033143

DEDICATION

To Bishop George W. Brooks, senior pastor of Mount Zion Baptist Church, in Greensboro, North Carolina. Without your faith and trust in both of us and our work, obviously this book never could have been written. Thank you!

To Beverly and Cate, our wives. Thanks for your love and patience!

To the past and present students, staff, and board of Welfare Reform Liaison Project—your spirit and hard work made this organization an easy place to love!

To Oren Rawls, whose editorial suggestions were terrific!

Many thanks to Alan Brilliant, our great indexer.

CONTENTS

PREFACE

I never thought I'd be cowriting a book less than five years after the day in 2006 when I found myself—a preacher from little old Greensboro, North Carolina—sitting in the John F. Kennedy School of Government at Harvard University.

I had enrolled in Harvard Divinity School's 2006 Summer Leadership Institute, along with about fifty other individuals from across the country. The executive training program is for clergy, lay leaders, and community activists who are involved in faith-based community and economic development. Over the course of two weeks, we all were required to complete an action plan related to our work in our own local community.

Preston Noah Williams, Houghton Research Professor of Theology and Contemporary Change at Harvard, directed the Summer Leadership Institute. And he was serious! I did not see Dr. Williams smile for the first three or four days that we were in Cambridge. We attended lectures, seminars, forums, field visits, and worship services. Because the workload was so demanding and exhausting, we had to remain free from all outside responsibilities and distractions during the two weeks.

In the first couple of days I struggled to grasp the process of preparing an action plan. Believe me, it was going to be done exactly as Dr. Williams outlined.

A few times the quiet voice in the back of my mind asked, "Odell, do you belong here? Odell, are you able to compete at this level?" Yes, I had been invited to attend. Yes, I had completed and submitted the application. Yes, I had been accepted into this world at Harvard. Yes, I had been able to pay the $5,000 tuition, with help from Skip Moore, president of the Weaver Foundation, which has been a key supporter of my own agency, the Welfare Reform Liaison Project. Yes, I had crossed the Charles River—but I still didn't know whether I belonged or whether I could compete at this level. This was Harvard, after all, and this program was for real!

I stayed up until four in the morning every day, studying and reading, increasingly convincing myself that I belonged. I knew quite well that I was not one of the book-smartest individuals in the class, so I was determined to outwork the others. In my dozen-plus years running the Welfare Reform Liaison Project, I've met plenty of people who are smarter than I am but not many who work as hard as I have in learning to build a successful agency.

Then, on the morning of the fourth day, something amazing happened. Dr. Williams introduced the class to the case-study method of teaching. The case method helped me fully understand action plans in the context of other agencies and organizations. Hallelujah! Praise the Lord! My prayers were answered. On that day, the educational instruction became focused on a set of case studies about faith-based institutions, corporations, and the transformation of communities. Many of the cases illustrated how to attract resources for building effective for-profit and nonprofit institutions and for strengthening the economic and moral infrastructure of neighborhoods.

The case studies were exciting for me because the idea behind them is exactly what my agency, Welfare Reform Liaison Project Inc., has been about from the beginning. They were also exciting for me because, even though I'd never heard the term *case study* before, Dr. Robert Wineburg had been mentoring me for the previous ten years along the same lines. The Harvard Law School had begun substituting case studies for classroom lectures as early as 1871. All I knew was that the method's name was new to me, but not the method itself.

Dr. Wineburg—"Wine," as I now call him—the Jefferson Pilot Excellence Professor in the Department of Social Work at the University of North Carolina at Greensboro, had drilled the case-study method of learning into me. He would always point out how an agency had succeeded or why a certain person had failed in exactly the same case-study manner that I was facing at the Summer Leadership Institute.

Yes, I belonged! Yes, I could compete—thanks to ten years of mentoring from Dr. Wineburg.

I immediately understood the "game," so for me, it was game on! In business and sports I was competitive, and I realized that, in this academic setting, I was more than qualified for a hands-on approach. My brain already operated that way. All of a sudden, the Summer Leadership Institute was paradise.

The institute had four modules: (1) theology, ethics, and public policy; (2) organizational development and management; (3) housing and community development; and (4) finance and economic development. After studying them, I felt very good about 2, 3, and 4. I was well prepared: I had already done an undergraduate degree in business, and I had twenty years of business experience and ten years of experience developing and running the Welfare Reform Liaison Project. However, I knew the module on theology, ethics, and public policy could cause a problem for me if I weren't careful. I am not a pulpit preacher or an ethicist or a big policy guy.

So I developed a game plan: I would always raise my hand first for any questions dealing with the second, third, or fourth modules, knowing that if I did so, the instructors would not call on me for questions about the first module. I didn't want them to ask me anything about the first module, but I wanted them to know that I was well versed in all of the other modules. As the days proceeded, I realized that the instructors had started to ignore my raised hand, especially when I began answering too many of the questions or making too many comments. The plan had worked!

We studied and evaluated numerous case studies involving various national leaders and their organizations. Then, in the final days of the program, those same leaders came to class, presented their cases, and told us what actually happened and why. Here are just a few of the leaders who came: Reverend Dr. Charles Gilchrist Adams, Hartford Memorial Baptist Church in Detroit; Dr. Laura Morgan Roberts, assistant professor of organizational behavior at the Harvard Business School; Dr. Lula Bailey Ballton, executive director of the West Angeles Community Development Corporation in Los Angeles; and Reverend Dr. Floyd Flake, senior pastor of the Greater Allen African Methodist Church in New York.

Dr. Williams smiled a lot during the presentations. It was clear that, over the years, he had developed a special relationship with many of those who were presenting. I fully understood the value of those special relationships: they reminded me very much of the relationship that has developed between Wine and me. About halfway through the program, Dr. Williams said that one of us might some day develop a program worthy of becoming a case study at the Summer Leadership Institute. My quiet inner voice, which just a week earlier had asked whether I belonged, now was saying, "I have a program right now that will be a case study one day." Indeed, what Wine and I offer readers in the pages ahead is the case study that was born at the institute in 2006. (My, my: it's amazing what one will say when his confidence returns!)

At the Summer Leadership Institute, I regained my confidence and competitive side—the one I had as an athlete and a salesperson. And it was a pleasure and an honor to be sitting in those seats, learning from some of the best professors in the world. I felt humbled and privileged to be in that class. One of the requirements of the institute was to have an action plan that included three of the four modules. The four best action plans would be presented to the class and staff on the last day of the institute. I felt that I could prepare an action plan with a chance of being selected as a finalist. That sudden urge to compete for one of the spots consumed me. I was at Harvard, and I didn't just want to compete—I wanted to win! No surprise, the Welfare Reform Liaison Project was my action plan—and it was selected as a finalist. I stayed up all night going over my presentation, over and over and over again. In the morning, I presented my action plan with incredible passion, and I challenged faith leaders to do more than just preach inside the four walls of our churches.

In the presentation, I talked about training students at my agency's Job Training Distribution Center to address workforce development on site. I pointed out how we made money and put it back into stipends for our students, and I mentioned our biennial Faith Summit. I talked about our Holy Hook Up, a program in which we take merchandise to the public housing community much like library bookmobiles do. The projects won national awards for us together with the United Way of Greater Greensboro from the Department of Housing and Urban Development.

During the question-and-answer portion of my presentation, there were few questions. The other people in the classroom were looking at me as if to say, "Who are you?" Remember, I am from Greensboro, North Carolina—just a community in the upper South—not from Boston, New York, Chicago, or Ann Arbor. But I knew who I was, and I knew that my action plan was solid. I also knew that, though there was a lot for me to learn at Harvard, there was also a thing or two my agency could teach ivory-tower academics.

The story told in the following chapters has a thing or two to teach academics as well. In just a dozen years, the Welfare Reform Liaison Project went from an idea—my master's thesis "Some Black Churches' Response to the 1996 Welfare Reform Act"—to a nationally recognized workforce development corporation. Today, I try to win for the poor—doing so is my religious calling. The Greensboro community and many special people have shaped and molded my drive, and that's what a large part of this book is about. I am proud to be in this competition, and this book reflects that pride.

Trust me—my agency wouldn't be anywhere close to where it is today if it weren't for my friendship with Dr. Robert Wineburg. Along the way, Wine and I have taught each other a lot. He has been my everyday Harvard, and I've been his regular case study. It is a special story that we have to tell, and it's one we both tell with pride. I hope readers gain as much from reading our story as we have in telling it.

In His Service,
Odell Cleveland
Greensboro, North Carolina, August 2, 2010

Introduction

CURRENT STATUS OF THE WELFARE REFORM LIAISON PROJECT

This is the story of Reverend Odell Cleveland and myself, Bob Wineburg. It is told in my voice, but the words written here are both of ours. The book generally follows five periods over more than thirteen years: (1) start-up, from 1996 to 1998; (2) establishment of roots in the community, from 1999 to 2001; (3) expansion, from 2002 to 2003; (4) stabilization, from 2004 to 2006; and (5) becoming an integral part and leader in Greensboro's human services community, from 2007 to the present. The book is a narrative, so at times we do not follow that timeline exactly. The story itself is about community and all that means, so events at one time shaped those at another. Thus, by weaving in and out of the timeline, we thought we could give the best picture of this complex and unbelievable but true story.

Odell is the president and chief executive officer of the Welfare Reform Liaison Project Inc., a faith-based nonprofit workforce development agency in Greensboro, North Carolina. I am a professor at the Greensboro campus of the University of North Carolina.

As might be expected from the state that raised Michael Jordan, Odell and I first met on the basketball court. We recount that story, and others, in the coming pages, but first a word about why we deem our story worth telling. Today, the Welfare Reform Liaison Project is a nationally recognized agency, having earned acclaim from churches, nonprofits, and corporations alike. But it didn't even exist fifteen years ago, and when Odell first conceived of what would become the agency, it was nothing more than an abstract idea.

The story of how we got to here from there is an unlikely one, but it offers several commonsense lessons for achieving long-term programmatic success in the nonprofit world. Our story covers the agency's growth since 1997, including the ups and downs in its developmental cycle. It is a story about an agency's position in the social services community and about the agency's increasingly complex relations with the broader Greensboro community and the nation beyond—religious congregations, corporations, philanthropies, government, media—as well as with those it aims to serve, the economically disadvantaged.

This book avoids most discussion of greater social forces, though at times they are relevant to understanding the development of the Welfare Reform Liaison Project. Policy changes, economic upheaval, and organizational development of course shape the story line of this book, but they are not the focus here. This is a story, told in straightforward language, of how an agency in one community grew to help its poor become self-sufficient. And it's the story of Odell's personal and organizational successes and his stumbles on the way up, and the supporting role I had in that process.

As we start the book, we ask readers to keep several things in mind. Many chapters feature a vignette, an e-mail, or a document. We have included them to show that people, organizations, and community institutions are both masters of their fates and servants of their destiny, often simultaneously. We hope these things enhance the story—we have not included them to prove a point necessarily.

We have strived to reconstruct events accurately enough to declare them facts. We are both pack rats and have kept everything, so we have more than a dozen years of documentation on which to base this story.

Chapter 1 begins where it logically should: at the beginning, thirteen years ago. So here we felt it appropriate to offer a current description of the agency and its programs. Today, the Welfare Reform Liaison Project is a multiservice workforce development corporation with a seventy-two-thousand-square-foot operation at the Nussbaum Business Center in Greensboro, North Carolina.

In 2010, the agency had enrollment of 196 low-income students, with an average age of twenty-three years, in its program, up from 147 the previous year. Figure 1 offers a demographic breakdown of the Welfare Reform Liaison Project's students. Nearly all live below the poverty level, and most are African American. More than a third were recently homeless.

The program enrollment is split evenly between men and women. The students are jobless and have few employable skills. At the Welfare Reform Liaison Project, they undergo rigorous training, often for the first time, to have a better chance at landing a low-paying job. But they graduate with knowledge, skills, and the ability to do things in those entry-level positions that will allow them to build a lasting work history.

Most graduates of the Welfare Reform Liaison Project leave with a better chance of growing than they had when they first walked through its doors. The Welfare Reform Liaison Project's success in helping people reach self-sufficiency is due to the quality of the training it provides, the support it offers to its students, and its innovative combinations of program activities.

The core of the agency's training revolves around courses on personal growth and development, entry-level management, media, and digital records. These classroom courses are conducted alongside intense on-the-job training in the Welfare

Gender		Age		Race	
Female:	98	17 or under:	2	Black:	165
		18–23:	27	White:	23
Male:	98	24–44:	107	Hispanic:	2
		45–54:	46	Native American:	0
		55–69:	13	Asian:	2
		70+:	1	Other:	2
Total:	196	Total:	196	Total:	194

Level of Income		Source of Income		Education	
$0–10,830:	179	Employment:	32	0–8:	9
$10,831–14,570:	3	Work First:	4	9–12 attended (nongraduate):	8
$14,571–18,310:	5	SSI:	2	GED:	43
$18,311–22,050:	5	Social Security:	2	High school graduate:	98
$22,051–25,790:	3	Pension:	0	College (nongraduate):	21
$25,791–29,530:	0	Unempl. comp.:	9	College/tech. school graduate:	17
$29,531–33,270:	1	No income:	23		
$33,271–37,010+:	0	Other:	0		

Family Type		Family Size		Other Characteristics	
Single parent (female):	47	1:	149	Food stamp recipient:	21
Single parent (male):	8	2:	22	Medicaid recipient:	1
Two-parent household:	8	3:	13	Subsidized housing:	0
Single person:	108	4:	9	Own:	33
Two adults (no children):	5	5:	2	Rent:	82
Other:	15	6:	1	Homeless:	78
		7:	0	No health insurance:	158
		8+:	0	Handicapped:	2
				Veteran:	0
				Farmer:	0
				Seasonal farmworker:	0
				Migrant farmworker:	0

FIGURE 1. *Demographic Breakdown of the Welfare Reform Liaison Project's Students*

Reform Liaison Project's corporate-quality distribution center (we will speak much more about the distribution center later in this book).

All who enter through the Welfare Reform Liaison Project's doors receive case management services and follow-up consultations, because program participants face far more than just professional challenges. Along with psychological concerns, they have to overcome the obstacles of day-to-day life: child care or finding shelter for the night.

Program participants go through an assessment and evaluation process when they first become involved with the Welfare Reform Liaison Project. This enables agency staff to ascertain which problems students face in their lives and how those problems may hinder their successful completion of the program. The assessment also helps shape the important partnerships between agency resources and student efforts, in that case management services hinge on good collaboration with agencies that provide what students need to succeed in the program but that the program does not offer, like child care.

The Welfare Reform Liaison Project's self-sufficiency-oriented program provides training in a variety of soft and hard skills, from interpersonal communication to money management. What has truly set the agency apart, however, is its Job Training Distribution Center.

The Welfare Reform Liaison Project has agreements with several corporations to receive new donated merchandise, which forms the bulk of the inventory at the distribution center. This warehouse offers an invaluable opportunity to train program participants in areas such as stocking, customer service, and the development of good work habits. The warehouse also provides a secondary benefit to the broader community because faith-based organizations and nonprofit agencies use merchandise from the warehouse to assist their beneficiaries and meet agencies' needs.

Many program participants have personal or work histories that make it difficult for them to secure a job. One way to change such an outcome is to offer participants the chance to learn the skills they need to establish their own businesses or serve in management positions. At the Welfare Reform Liaison Project, this effort has two tracks.

Participants selected for the entrepreneurial program enroll in American Management Association certificate classes. This series of six classes provides basic skills needed for business management and personnel supervision. As we write this, the Welfare Reform Liaison Project is moving to make the American Management Association classes an in-house certificate program.

The second track consists of training in an area that can result in the ability to establish a small business or to acquire independent contractor status. The Welfare Reform Liaison Project has developed a video production and graphic creation and design program. This program provides materials—graphics for films, DVDs, public service announcements, and other digital media—for public agencies, private nonprofit organizations, and faith institutions while also providing students with an opportunity to develop marketable skills.

Students learn digital photography skills, for use in presentations and written materials such as annual reports, as well as video production, including storyboarding, videography, and interviewing techniques. The students' work has been used for a number of productions for different publics. The curriculum consists of training developed by the Welfare Reform Liaison Project, using local experts and training provided by Guilford Technical Community College.

The uniqueness of the agency's program is the integration of classroom training with simulated job experience, small business development, and management assistance. To accomplish this, the agency has partnered with a broad range of Greensboro institutions—the community college, the chamber of commerce, local employers, and many others. In addition, the Welfare Reform Liaison Project has developed partnerships with several other organizations and programs that provide job-training activities for people with developmental disabilities, the Latino community, and those participating in the Department of Social Services' Work First program (more commonly known as the welfare-to-work program).

The Welfare Reform Liaison Project has fifteen full-time staff members and three part-time job developers, who were hired as a result of the receipt of federal stimulus funds from the American Recovery and Reinvestment Act. In addition, in 2009, 1,626 different volunteers logged a total of 13,260 hours. Volunteers performed more than twelve thousand of those hours of service at the Job Training Distribution Center.

The volunteer hours themselves amount to the equivalent of 1.3 full-time staff members, but they offer much more value than just time. The volunteers represent the many community institutions that have used the Welfare Reform Liaison Project so members from churches and civic organizations can live out part of their own organizations' charitable missions.

Those twelve thousand volunteer hours, and tens of thousands more put in by trainees at the Job Training Distribution Center, primarily involve working with donated corporate goods. This part of the Welfare Reform Liaison Project's operations is central to our story, and we'll discuss it in greater depth in a later chapter. In brief, the distribution center allows companies that might otherwise discard goods that they no longer sell to donate them instead to charity for a greater tax write-off. The growing list of companies that have partnered with the Welfare Reform Liaison Project includes some of the biggest names in corporate America, among them Wal-Mart, Men's Wearhouse, RadioShack, and CVS.

Odell, who used to be in the trucking business, figured out a way to get bulk donated goods to Greensboro cheaply. Once the items arrive at the Welfare Reform Liaison Project, they are sorted, repackaged, and redistributed. Trainees do all of this work.

For example, Men's Wearhouse ships new suits that no longer sell in its market but still are fashionable. Upon arrival, trainees take off the labels and prepare the suits for shipping to agencies and organizations that have a market for those suits. It is financially imprudent for Men's Wearhouse to ship these suits offshore and then ship them back for redistribution and pay for "delabeling." The tax laws are such that nonprofit donations can increase a company's bottom line more if they work domestically than internationally. The domestic social benefits, of course, are far greater as well.

The agency also contracts with toy companies for certain toys that no longer sell. Instead of dumping them, the companies ship them unsorted and in bulk to the Welfare Reform Liaison Project. The project has a partnership with Ronald McDonald Houses to sort the toys and distribute them back to individual Ronald McDonald Houses for kids to play with during their recovery.

The Welfare Reform Liaison Project's partnerships have come in all different shapes and sizes. For example, CVS wanted to donate sanitary kits to the victims of Hurricane Katrina in 2005. The pharmacy chain shipped the goods to Greensboro, where agency volunteers and students sorted, packaged, and redistributed them to New Orleans.

Salvation Army partners with the training side of the Welfare Reform Liaison Project by sending some of its shelter residents to the Job Training Distribution Center for work experience. Meanwhile, thirty-five public and nonprofit agencies and eighty-two religious congregations have a Sam's Club–like membership with the distribution center—nonprofits pay a yearly membership fee that allows them access to deeply discounted merchandise—which serves families in need of toiletries, cosmetics, and other items that food stamps do not cover. And a local coalition that seeks classroom donations from local businesses like Office Depot contracts for space at the distribution center where teachers can come and get classroom supplies for free. Students in the training program stock the shelves and keep them looking businesslike.

It is not only the community's most unfortunate, however, who gain on-the-job experience at the distribution center. The Welfare Reform Liaison Project serves as the broker for thirty-seven AmeriCorps Vista volunteers who are serving at the agency and at twenty-three other community organizations. And there are currently sixty-two student interns from area colleges. What is noteworthy is that six of them are from the state school where I teach, the University of North Carolina at Greensboro. They are in the business school's social entrepreneur program, helping with a business plan for a new digital record-keeping training program that is now being tested.

It is even more noteworthy that another forty-two students are from a business program at North Carolina Agricultural and Technical State University. They are working with a job developer to find more openings for trainees from the Welfare Reform Liaison Project. There have also been social work, political science, divinity, criminal justice, sociology, communications, and program-evaluation students who have served as interns at various times from colleges and universities across the region.

These are just a few of the seventy-four formal partnerships the Welfare Reform Liaison Project has cemented over the past thirteen years. Each partnership delivers double the bang per buck: the broader community benefits from the services of the Welfare Reform Liaison Project, and the project's trainees benefit from guided on-the-job training experience.

The Welfare Reform Liaison Project's annual budget is $1,365,000. More than a third of the budget, $466,000, comes from contracting and administrative fees earned at the Job Training Distribution Center. Copycents, the video production unit, brought in $31,000 in the past fiscal year through fees for producing videos for non-profit organizations. Cash donations accounted for $3,300, and another $12,000 came from the AmeriCorps Vista program. The remainder of the budget derives from a Community Service Block Grant, a yearly federal grant, and other smaller grants for which the Welfare Reform Liaison Project qualifies as a community action agency, a designation we discuss in detail in a later chapter.

We would be remiss if we didn't note that, in 2010, the Welfare Reform Liaison Project received $1.2 million in funding under the American Recovery and Reinvestment Act. The project allocated money from President Barack Obama's federal stimulus package, a onetime grant, to job-development programs that trained people for work quickly.

At an agency the size of the Welfare Reform Liaison Project—its outsize presence in the community notwithstanding—a grant like that can open up all sorts of opportunities as well as challenges. As of this writing, the project is implementing new and expanded programming, the long-term impact on Greensboro yet to be determined. Appendix 1 shows the agency's ongoing goals, as outlined in the application for the stimulus funds.

We would also be remiss if we didn't make clear how joint authorship of this book took place. I (Bob) did the writing, except for the preface. For the first two chapters, Odell and I spoke often about how to start out and what to include. I wrote a draft and sent it to Odell. He made comments, additions, and clarifications, and he added his own perspective. He then sent the draft back to me, and I wove his ideas into the text. After I made those changes, I sent it back to Odell, and he made yet more changes of his own.

After the first two chapters, we consulted often—sometimes I needed more information or clarification, and he would provide those through e-mail or directly by phone. After I finished the draft, Odell came over to my house and read the draft in my presence, making notes and changes, and asking questions. Many times throughout this effort, we sat over primary documents and reconstructed the events as we saw them—agreeing to disagree and agreeing that only what we both agreed on would go onto paper. We did this late into the evenings for many nights until we got every word the way we felt the story actually happened. At times we argued, especially around framing the racial issues; at other times, we laughed, looking at how far we had come with thirteen years together under our belts. Still other times we both looked at each other in disbelief—the story is, at times, simply unbelievable, but it is true. During the course of writing the book, at times I moved explicitly into my thinking about how I might approach something with Odell. We went over these aspects and agreed that they should be part of the story. One example of this occurs in chapter 5, though only briefly. I had said to Odell at least fifty times in the course of three years, "You need a Fred Newman," as I simply kept thinking that this organization needed someone that could bring excellence in daily internal matters much like Odell did in external affairs.

Our book is written in my voice, as one of us must unavoidably play the narrator. It was hard to write this and be part of the story. But the thoughts on which we have based the book are ours jointly. What follows, then, is our story. It is a good one.

CHAPTER 1

The $25,000 Home Run

A successful community organization today—how it got there in thirteen years is a story as instructive as it is unlikely. This chapter is about our relationship, how it began, public policy, preorganizational development, and starting a faith-based organization birthed from the spiritual womb of Mount Zion Baptist Church, one of the largest African-American churches between Washington, D.C., and Atlanta.

ODELL TODAY

To those in the know in Greensboro, a quick glance at the names of the members of the board of directors of United Way of Greater Greensboro reveals the community's movers and shakers (figure 2). These are exactly the kind of people a fund-raising, grant-making, and community-planning organization wants around the board table, the kind of people one is likely to find on the boards of many of the 1,485 United Ways around the country. Odell is the only minister and nonprofit agency director on the list.

Odell is now a fixture in the community, but barely a dozen years ago, he was an unordained minister with an embryonic storefront-like ministry. That he would rise to such a position in Greensboro was part of our strategy from the beginning. It had to be. Greensboro was an unforgiving environment for an upstart like the Welfare Reform Liaison Project, and intertwining Odell's agenda with that of the community was, by necessity, a key part of our mission.

We both played college sports and knew in our guts that the time was right for what we considered then swinging for the fences—a homerun, the big one, the game changer. And so Odell and I crafted a grant proposal for $25,000 from the Bryan Venture Grant Fund of the United Way to launch what has become today a nationally recognized workforce development organization.

CREATING THE COMMUNITY STORY: 1997

The $25,000 grant, which we received in 1997, was for a simple needs assessment, but it had a fancy name: the Faith Intervention and Connections Program. In reality, the grant was for research, something for which local funders don't easily hand out

Chuck Flynt
Chair, Board of Directors
Flynt Amtex Inc.

Jason P. Bohrer
United Guaranty Corporation

Dr. Janice G. Brewington
Community Volunteer

Mike Bumpass
First Point Inc./GMA

Michelle Gethers Clark
Community Volunteer

Sanders Cockman
Merrill Lynch

Sonya Conway
American Express

John Cross
Brooks, Pierce, McLendon,
Humphrey & Leonard, LLP

Mona G. Edwards
Center for Creative
Leadership

Valdemar Fischer
Syngenta

Kim Gatling
Smith Moore Leatherwood
LLP

Darby Henley
Merrill Lynch

Ed Kitchen
Joseph M. Bryan Foundation

Paul Mason
VF Corporation

Bobby Mendez
Ecolab Global Retail

Pressley A. Ridgill
NewBridge Bank

Judy Schanel
Moses Cone Health System

Sue D. White
Donathan Properties, Inc.

Otis Wilson
Community Volunteer
Keith E. Barsuhn
President, United Way of
Greater Greensboro

Dr. Linda P. Brady
University of North Carolina
at Greensboro

Tina Akers Brown
Greensboro Housing
Authority

Jeff Burgess
Grant Thornton, LLP

**REVEREND
ODELL CLEVELAND
WELFARE REFORM LIAISON
PROJECT INC., CAA**

Sue Cole
Granville Capital, Inc.

Mary Wood Copeland
Bell Partners, Inc.

J. Nathan Duggins, III
Tuggle, Duggins & Meschan,
PA

Monte Edwards
SRS, Inc.

Cecelia Foy-Dorsett
Senn Dunn Insurance

Joyce Gorham-Worsley
Greensboro Chamber of
Commerce

Randall Kaplan
The Capsule Group, LLC

Jennifer L. J. Koenig
Schell Bray Aycock Abel &
Livington PLLC

M. L. (Lee) McAllister
Iaver Investment Company

Ronald S. Milstein
Lorillard Tobacco Company

Robin A. Saul
News & Record

Laurie Iaver
Our State Magazine/Mann
Media

Susan L. Williams
VF Corporation

Dr. Terry Worrell
Guilford County Schools

Kristen Yntema
Advanced Home Care

FIGURE 2. *Board of Directors, United Way of Greater Greensboro*

money. I had chaired the Bryan Venture Grant Fund's allocation committee years before, so I had some insight into how the fund operated. We buried the research in a narrative that proposed to connect Odell with eighty-two mainly black pastors in the community to see what their churches were doing to address welfare reform.

I knew the local social services culture and the committee's ways from the vantage point of an engaged scholar who had been in the community and had done research about its service activities. So Odell had to "connect" so he wouldn't duplicate efforts—he had to learn what services other congregations were providing to learn whether they were considering other efforts like his—and he had to have proof that he was not doing so.

In reality, I didn't want him to get blindsided for being the new kid on the block and have his efforts torpedoed before he even set sail. The rumors and gossip that lace a community's system of services and are part of its everyday culture also include part of the daily service narrative, regardless of how true or false they may be. The running narrative is part of the reality that can grow into a horror story if it is not managed. Rumors and gossip usually are grounded, at least in small-town Greensboro, in tiny grains of truth, but they quickly become the story line if they aren't held in check.

I ultimately wanted Odell to show up at meetings as a familiar face in the community, not as stranger. Too much was at stake. Odell didn't know the grant game, and he could not conceive of the fact that his ministerial brethren could sink his God-inspired idea, which he prefers to call a vision, through community gossip, innuendo, and misinformation. He needed data to plan his program, and he needed contacts to form partnerships and avoid misinformation. He had to shape the story before others shaped it for him. Community gossip, though, can also be positive, and we wanted to create good first impressions and word-of-mouth advertisers, and have facts to back them up.

The story we shaped was of a rapidly growing organization best characterized as an institutional lazy Susan, in that it offered various appetizing offerings to the diverse organizations and businesses at Greensboro's communal table. The lesson of our story is, to paraphrase John Donne, that no institution is an island. No community organization can thrive if it stays isolated from the rest of the organizations in a community's sisterhood of care.

I believe that organizations should be built from the bottom up, the slow and steady way, with research and a strong vision at the core. Undoubtedly, there must be a strong implementation plan that the organization reviews and revises routinely. But the fulcrum around which everything revolves is the fact that successful community organizations build assets in the community and build from the assets in the community.

The Welfare Reform Liaison Project is certainly a successful community organization today. How it got there is a story as instructive as it is unlikely. Odell has always been guided by his vision, by his deep faith in God and in human potential, and by a contagious swagger and smile that come with knowing how to win. In contrast, I am guided by a commitment to intense study before action, a deep conviction that a slow and steady pace with controlled bursts of speed wins long races, and the adherence to the principle that the fewer degrees of separation between an organization and its potential community partners, the stronger the organization will be. Ours was hardly the making of a perfect partnership, but over time we grew to appreciate and trust the reality of the other's position.

The Welfare Reform Liaison Project had a university research partner from the beginning, Odell had a friend and adviser from the academy, and I had a friend who welcomed me into his agency and church at any time for any reason. What a laboratory!

COMPLETELY DIFFERENT BACKGROUNDS?

Before delving into the development of the Welfare Reform Liaison Project, I ought to first mention how Odell and I met. What started out as an uneventful inquiry on his part still provides a common language for our ongoing and fruitful relationship. But I want to first provide a snapshot of our backgrounds, because having that information will help you understand that two people traveling from different places, on completely different paths, found enough in common not just to forge a lasting friendship but also to develop a nonprofit that is central to their community's social service operation, one that is truly a national model for successful workforce development.

Odell and I are undoubtedly from different backgrounds, religions, and academic preparation, but our souls are in the same place—we care about the plight of the poor. Plus, for both of us, an overabundance of athletics shaped our formative years, so neither of us likes to lose—in fact, we hate it. Both of us had it drilled into us that it is not whether you win or lose; it is how you play the game.

For us, playing the game well, practicing hard, giving 100 percent all the time, regardless of the score, usually means being a pacesetter and winning more often than not. The poor don't win much, so we both wanted to do something in our small space on the planet to change the game so that the poor could win now and then. Being able to document the fact that, in Greensboro and surrounding Guilford County, so-called economic castoffs—ex-prisoners, ex–welfare moms, ex-prostitutes, immigrants, and the disabled—had earned $7 million since 1997 and had contributed to the tax base instead of draining it, is one testimony of Welfare Reform Liaison Project's success.

For Odell, a deeply religious man, the verses from Matthew 25:31–46 are guiding words for his agency. But before anyone jumps to conclusions about him being just another a Bible-thumping pastor blinded by faith, it is important to set the parameters of Odell's religious soul. For Odell, the verses from Matthew can be operationalized in one sentence: everyone—saint and sinner alike—deserves a second chance.

> When the Son of Man comes in his glory, and all the angels with him, he will sit on his throne in heavenly glory. All the nations will be gathered before him, and he will separate the people one from another as a shepherd separates the sheep from the goats. He will put the sheep on his right and the goats on his left.
>
> Then the King will say to those on his right, "Come, you who are blessed by my Father; take your inheritance, the kingdom prepared for you since the creation of the world. For I was hungry and you gave me something to eat, I was thirsty and you gave me something to drink, I was a stranger and you invited me in, I needed clothes and you clothed me, I was sick and you looked after me, I was in prison and you came to visit me."
>
> Then the righteous will answer him, "Lord, when did I see you hungry and feed you, or thirsty and give you something to drink? When did I see you a stranger and invite you in, or needing clothes and clothe you? When did I see you sick or in prison and go to visit you?"
>
> The King will reply, "I tell you the truth, whatever you did for one of the least of these brothers of mine, you did for me."
>
> Then he will say to those on his left, "Depart from me, you who are cursed, into the eternal fire prepared for the devil and his angels. For I was hungry and you gave me nothing to eat, I was thirsty and you gave me nothing to drink, I was a stranger and you did not invite me in, I needed clothes and you did not clothe me, I was sick and in prison and you did not look after me."
>
> They also will answer, "Lord, when did we see you hungry or thirsty or a stranger or needing clothes or sick or in prison, and did not help you?"
>
> He will reply, "I tell you the truth, whatever you did not do for one of the least of these, you did not do for me."
>
> Then they will go away to eternal punishment, but the righteous to eternal life.
>
> *—Matthew 25:31–40, New International Version*

Odell has built his ministry on that principle, has built relationships on that standard, and runs an organization on that code. From the time of Bill Clinton's pledge to "change welfare as we know it" through George W. Bush's faith-based initiatives and to this very day, Odell has been all about "doing" the Gospels.

Odell is all about second chances because his life has been full of them. As Odell puts it: "Imagine finding yourself twenty-five years old, a divorced mother of four, living in public housing working all day in a sewing factory and attending school at night pursuing your GED. While preparing to leave for work you have a massive stroke and hours later doctors and family members are discussing your chances of living or dying. Also, how the four children will be divided and cared for by the family. As she was dying, she asked God to allow her to live long enough to raise her children."

Odell's mother survived and raised her four children on a small disability check and a lot of faith and love. This combination ensured that all of her children earned college educations, as did she after the kids were grown. Odell was captain of a national basketball championship team in the National Association of Intercollegiate Athletics—a team leader whose dream of making the NBA was shattered when no contract appeared. He got a second chance in school, going an extra year and a half to complete a degree in business while working early-morning shifts at UPS. Had he majored in leisure studies like the coaches wanted, we never would have written this book.

Although Odell grew up poor, his business degree and the leadership abilities he honed on the basketball court landed him a position as a sales representative for a Greensboro-based trucking firm. He was one of the firm's top sales representatives in the country and the only black. He was making good money, but he prayed for more meaning in his life than sales awards could offer.

He leaped into the Hood Theological Seminary, an attempt at a second chance. As an athlete used to winning—South Carolina state high school basketball championship, NAIA national collegiate basketball championship, and the hundreds of winning games that got him there—winning at selling trucking contracts just could not nourish Odell's longing for more purpose. The ministry was Odell's second chance—and it turned out to be a way for him to give second chances to countless others.

Odell has a certain sermon he gives on the ministry circuit, the same one he gives to his students in his training classes—he calls it "Why Is It So Expensive to Be Poor?" He doesn't talk about the financial aspects of being poor—though he has been known to joke, "I was so po' that I couldn't afford the o and the r." Rather, he focuses on the currency that poverty extracts from one's soul once a person lets being down and out take over the never-quit attitude, the belief that he or she can make a second chance work. Odell knows the drawing down of poverty's quicksand.

There is no question that when Odell talks about his rise up in life, he is talking about what he learned in his personal transformation of giving his life over to Jesus Christ. But he doesn't use that language these days, because he is a true believer in faith works, a principle of action based on one's faith. Odell's message is about the costs that demons extract from a person when they take over one's everyday life. Odell helps people chase away their inner demons so that they can get a grip on their inner possibilities. He knows about what he talks—he has chased demons away many times.

Although there is no question that Odell prayed hard for a second chance to move from the corporate world to the ministry, many working principles besides prayer came into play to make his organization a success over the past thirteen years. The first was that Odell is a visionary.

Often called an originator in leadership scholarship, Chris Musselwhite, president and CEO of Discovery Learning Inc., has developed a leadership training package in which he describes three kinds of leaders: the conserver, the pragmatist, and the originator. The conserver sees only the trees in the forest; the originator sees only the forest without the trees; and the pragmatist sees both the forest and the trees and can work, though sometimes constrained by visions that are too big or too small, with both the conserver and the originator. In a forest fire, a conserver puts out fires tree by tree, the originator goes outside of the box and puts a wet blanket over the whole fire, and the pragmatist devises a way to use the blanket on sections of trees that would redirect the fire to put it out without it spreading further.

Much goes into the psychological makeup of Odell Cleveland, more than I want or am qualified to talk about here. His growing up poor in the projects, his athletic discipline, his mother's near-death experience, his deep faith, and much more are all factors that make Odell who he is—a visionary with a heart and deeply religious soul. But organizations limp along or fail without the right leader at the right time who does the right things. In taking the skills he gained in corporate America and applying them to help change poor people's lives through the ministry, Odell needed something more to contribute to his second-chance mission: a pragmatist, someone who could ground the Welfare Reform Liaison Project in well-researched, well-established, well-practiced organizational principles.

That's where I come into the picture. My background has little of the flavor, poignancy, or struggle of Odell Cleveland's. I grew up in a working-class, two-parent household, not very religious but very Jewish and in a distinctly Jewish neighborhood. I was never the student my older and younger brothers were. They were Ivy League undergraduates and earned advanced degrees at Cornell and Stanford, respectively. My route reflected that of a more typical working-class person of my era—

community college and then college. I never imagined I would have an advanced degree, let alone two. To earn a sense of self in my Jewish community—when Sandy Koufax was as much a hero as Albert Einstein—I played basketball in high school and played baseball, my first love, in college.

But Odell and I hardly came from different planets. While I was growing up in Utica, New York, our family business was a mom-and-pop shop in the ghetto, across the street from the projects. As a kid, I walked through the heart of the ghetto on Saturday nights to catch the bus back to the Jewish 'hood and never quite understood why my friends asked me whether doing so scared me. I was allowed to play basketball on the courts in the projects and was often invited because I was "Bennie's boy." When my father Bennie died, there were as many black people at the funeral as white. In 1968, when race riots started to hit my city and many others, the community members spared our family store from the riots.

Early on, Odell wasn't completely ready to trust me—the white, Jewish professor—but he liked my style. Race in America is a big deal on the macrolevel, and we both knew it. However, in the trenches of daily Greensboro human services activity—where leaders are primarily white but many agency staff are black and work daily with black people at the depths of poverty—where both of us are engaged, Odell didn't find any of the tiptoeing around race that white and black strangers often do around each other. I grew up in an era of tell it like it is—in the black community. As was Odell, I was racially bilingual. And as Odell likes to note, I was, unlike him, a member of the National Association for the Advancement of Colored People (NAACP).

In 1973, my wife and I, just three months after we were married, joined Volunteers in Service to America (Vista) and spent a life-changing year on the Blackfeet Indian Reservation in Montana. Seeing so much poverty, family violence, child neglect, and alcoholism daily burned my soul, and I decided to spend the rest of my life working in my small way to do something about poverty.

Although Odell and I, at least from thirty thousand feet, were unlikely to meet up, and even more unlikely to forge a lasting partnership, that's how it turned out. For Odell, it was God's will. For me, I followed my nose. It was not, however, love at first sight.

Odell saw divine intervention in our meeting—"Who was I to question why God put this bald-headed, Jewish professor into my life?" he so endearingly put it. My only personal relationship with God is a good argument every so often, so I saw our encounter through a rather different filter. When I saw the chance to be inside of a black church wrestling with practical issues regarding welfare reform, as an academic, I thought I would have to be crazy to pass up the opportunity. All of my former experiences, my promise to myself that I would do something about all the pain and suffering I had seen, and my interest in welfare policy as a student and professor gelled when I had the chance to work with Odell.

And so this story begins, as so much in North Carolina does, in a basketball locker room.

THE GYM

The simple story is that Odell and I met in the winter of 1997, in the locker room of Greensboro's Guilford College, where we and a bunch of others played hoops on Mondays, Wednesdays, and Fridays—and we still do, to this day. But nothing in relationships is simple.

I played basketball with an increasingly aging group of Guilford faculty and YMCA members (the Y and the college shared a gym and pool until seven years ago). Three games would be going on simultaneously, and those who showed up late migrated to the game with the fewest players. My game, which officially became known as the geezer game, was the least competitive and had the fewest players. Odell, who often came late, started to play regularly in the geezer game. He was in his midthirties then and was very good, a level above everyone else in the geezer game, and even playing with the twentysomethings. But instead of showing his expertise with the seniors, he made everyone around him in the senior game better. He played hard, and to win, but not with the win-or-die mentality that dominated the younger games. Asked why he half-jokingly and half-seriously called himself Moses on more than one occasion, the ever-confident Odell replied, "He could lead his team to the Promised Land."

Odell has the same mind-set about all of those who have passed through the doors of the Welfare Reform Liaison Project. Odell is on the United Way board today because, in thirteen years, every person, social service organization, business, and ministry he has touched has improved as a result of his personal and organizational style—and the community knows it.

Odell is a who's-who in the Greensboro social service community. Why? Because he puts ex-prisoners to work, and they stay out of jail. He helps prostitutes restore their self-respect and dignity by getting them through community college. Today, the disabled and developmentally disabled are part of his operation—they receive training and find a comfortable and safe environment at the Welfare Reform Liaison Project before entering the free job market. Jews, Muslims, whites, and blacks are welcome in his program equally, because Odell brings people to their self-designed Promised Lands. As the leader of his organization, he leads like he does on the basketball court; he creates an environment in which people can maximize their potential. That is powerful and rare leadership.

As a student of social policy, especially responses of state and local human services delivery systems to large shifts in policy, a true student of welfare policy since the Carter presidency, and trained in community organization as an MSW student at Syracuse University, I surprisingly found myself in many churches after Reagan cut the human services budget, strategizing with the community to help those hit by the cuts. There was nothing in the social work literature about congregations as community-based organizations, so I realized that was why I never studied anything about them as a graduate student. I learned later through my own digging that religious congregations in the academic world were the province of study in sociology of religion and community ministry programs in theology schools.

The 1980s shaped my academic path. When the Reagan budget cuts of the 1980s hit Greensboro and communities nationwide, I was interested in helping my community seek local solutions to eliminating some of the suffering people experienced from lost benefits. As a social work professor in a program that had a reputation for working in the community, I was called on to help by local agency leaders. I found myself in churches for those meetings. Like I said, the scholarly literature said nothing about congregations being community partners in social service provision. However, my research of local news stories around the country of congregational and community service collaboration told me that what I was finding in Greensboro was more than a local phenomenon. (In the early 1990s, the Lilly Endowment funded my research on this subject and I became one of the first academics to validate empirically that congregations were partners with social service organizations in caring for those in need in the community. I was the first scholar to look empirically, from the agency point of view, at how congregations plan for, implement, and evaluate the resources of the religious community. This work catapulted me and my Greensboro research into the national world of scholarship on faith-based social services. Until 2000, I received funding for this research from Lilly and a Lilly-funded subcontract with Yale University.) I kept searching the literature to find something about congregational service provision and congregations as community-based organizations that partnered generously with government and other nonprofit providers. Finding only crumbs of research and nothing about how social policy changes affect local religious responses, I decided to study what I saw playing out locally in the 1980s on my own, without academic guideposts but with essential community partners.

Fifteen years later, in the fall of 1997, and with several local studies and many articles behind me, I was invited to speak at Yale University on congregational responses to the welfare changes of 1996. Like the geneticist who gets a bead on the human genome system by studying the fruit fly, my community studies had enabled me to slowly unravel and make sense of the workings of community partnerships in relationship to program success. Community human services systems are more similar than different nationwide, but make no mistake, every community is different from ours in Greensboro.

In 1997, the University of North Carolina at Greensboro was a regional school in the state university system. A press release was worthy for a faculty member invited to Yale. One would seriously doubt that a local New Haven newspaper would mention that one of Yale's faculty was speaking at UNC Greensboro. That is the difference between a university with the national reach and one geared toward helping the local and regional communities.

At any rate, our local paper, the *Greensboro News and Record*, ran an innocuous little blurb noting my invitation. On the Friday following the news story, sitting next to each other in the locker room after the games, Odell opened the first conversation we had ever had. He graciously acknowledged my invitation to Yale. I liked the recognition, of course, because all minor leaguers like the chance to play in the big leagues, even for a day. The conversation evolved, and before I knew it, we had found common ground. I learned that he was making the transition to the ministry from selling trucking contracts by attending a part-time theology program at Hood Theological Seminary in Salisbury, North Carolina, fifty miles from Greensboro.

At the time, Odell was close to defending his master's thesis, "Some Black Churches' Response to the 1996 Welfare Reform Act," in which he outlined a prescriptive program that would help women transition from welfare to work. The topic was certainly in line with my research and the topic I was addressing at Yale.

THE THESIS

Odell had been through a mental ringer on his thesis. He did not understand that there were options, both thesis and nonthesis, as pathways to earning a master's degree in theology at Hood. He simply couldn't conceptualize a master's degree without a thesis. And by the time he learned that there were two options, he was too deep into the thesis option, and there was no turning back. He also learned that if he failed the thesis defense, there was no second chance to earn the master's degree at that institution. For Odell, succeeding at his defense was like being on the foul line with no time on the clock and one shot left to put the game in overtime. If he missed, he lost. Odell was nervous. He wanted some reinforcement that he was on the right track in his thesis, so he gave a draft of it to Bishop George W. Brooks, senior pastor of Mount Zion Baptist Church. The church's emergency assistance ministry was overwhelmed with requests for assistance, and it had a well-earned reputation in the broader network of community agencies for helping those whom no other agency could or would help. The church was also Odell's congregation, and it has grown to become one of the largest African-American churches between Washington, D.C., and Atlanta. Our examination of the Emergency Assistance Program's distribu-

20

PRACADEMICS AND COMMUNITY CHANGE

tion records showed that, in the nine years before the 1996 welfare reform and its implementation in 1997 and 1998, Mount Zion had distributed $379,000 to help people with food, rent, transportation, prescription drugs, child care, and the like. This generosity did not take into account the numerous on-site programs the church offered or the countless hours volunteers spent administering such programs. The figures merely show the cash outlay.

Of the people who received help, 70 percent were not members of the congregation. Even more surprising were the large expenditures of cash during 1996, 1997, and five months into 1998. In those years, the national narrative on welfare reform, and then the new law, scared people from going to the public agency and eliminated some people from the rolls. They sought help at Mount Zion's Emergency Assistance Program, and our data bear this out. The comments of our evaluator, Dr. Fasih Amhed of Carolina Evaluation, illustrate what was happening with Mount Zion's Emergency Assistance Program (EAP). Dr. Amhed was my "numbers man" for a three-year grant I received from the Lilly Endowment in 1991 to study social service partnerships between agencies and congregations in Greensboro.

It is noteworthy that a comprehensive and detailed accounting system is maintained for the EAP, not typical of most programs managed by volunteers. This evaluator was pleasantly surprised when resource input data for the last three years was quickly retrieved in the format required by him.

Direct emergency assistance of $80,050 and $84,150 was provided in 1996 and 1997 respectively, an annual increase of about 5%. Data for the first five months of 1998 indicates that if monthly average is maintained, the projected amount of assistance for the current year would be around $97,000, which may reflect an increase of about 15% over last year.

This trend of steady increase in the need for emergency assistance portends increasing strain on the church's resources to sustain the program. On the average EAP assists around 270 persons every year, and about 70% of recipients are not members of the church, which reflects relatively high level of accessibility to the program.

—**Dr. Fasih Amhed**, *evaluation of the Emergency Assistance Program,*
Mount Zion Baptist Church of Greensboro

Bishop Brooks was eager to build a nonprofit organization and get community support for a new crop of women who were being pushed off the welfare roles but were not making money to feed themselves or their families. He knew that what was becoming a national crisis for the poor and a local crisis for Mount Zion would overwhelm the church, and the crisis would reduce the church's overall emergency efforts if something more systemic weren't done through broader community development efforts.

Bishop Brooks may not have realized, or may not have wanted to know, that Odell was only seeking legitimacy for his academic ideas—he didn't really want to start a welfare to work ministry. Mount Zion had paid for Odell's schooling, and Odell banked on the fact that choosing a thesis topic, but it was just a thesis topic, that was relevant to black seminarians—welfare reform and the black church's response—would get him through successfully. Still, the idea was only academic to him at the time, and it enabled him to stay away from having to argue Scripture in his thesis. Instead, he could argue for a practical religious response to a looming national concern, especially in the black community: how churches would respond to the sea change in welfare reform. Odell never wanted to be a pulpit pastor. His approach was to become a community minister, or a pastor without a pew. To do this, his thesis presented a practical idea that would build from Mount Zion's Emergency Assistance Program. In his seminary program, his classmates labeled him a "social gospel preacher." Odell had showed the thesis to Bishop Brooks to prove that the money for his schooling was well spent in the academic sense; he had no intention of operationalizing his ideas. But Bishop Brooks did see real-life potential for the church to tackle a new and potentially large problem, and he asked Odell outright whether he could do what he outlined in the thesis. Odell asked me about his defense. I said he would push a peanut around with his nose, but once the committee members started arguing with themselves over welfare policy and the black church, he should keep his mouth shut. That is exactly what happened, and he kept his mouth shut for forty minutes.

At the time, Odell was making a good living, doing a good job supporting his wife and young family. Then suddenly he had the opportunity to build a ministry of his own—but it came before he was ready psychologically or financially. Spiritually, though, he was ready as ever. When Bishop Brooks read the thesis, he asked, "Can you do what you said on paper?" The subtext was this: "If this is good enough for you to get a master's degree, it is good enough for you to do at Mount Zion." Bishop Brooks then said, "If you take on the challenge of [developing the program in the thesis], the church will pay you a salary and expenses for the first year. And if you can't make it work within a year, I am going to personally fire you. Do you want the mission?" Odell responded, "I need to go home to talk to my wife and pray on it."

He and his wife faced a huge decision. Odell could tell the bishop, the man who would eventually ordain him, that he was just theorizing and had no intention of building the kind of ministry he proposed in his thesis. If he did that, he knew he'd lose face with his senior pastor and let down the poor women he had theorized about helping.

He could keep his well-paying job, or he could start on the road to the Promised Land but without much of a map. There would be far less money if he said yes to Bishop Brooks, but he would have Mount Zion's backing and ordination around the corner if he chose the riskier path. When I did follow up with Bishop Brooks in June 2010 about the first grant that he sent Odell to get from the United Way in 1997, he told me that he doesn't ever ordain ministers to become reverends unless they demonstrate that they can produce works, be it in the church or in the community, that are beyond what any parishioner can achieve. Ordained ministers represent the church, and both have a special mission. That mission is sanctified by ordination and is recognized both in the church and the broader community.

Odell and his wife, Beverly, are different from each other when it comes to risk taking. Odell takes risks; Beverly does not. She helps Odell stay focused and balanced. However, they both look for silver linings in gray clouds and are guided by a deep and genuine faith.

Beverly's only question to Odell was, "Is this God, or is it you?" Odell said he "believed it was God," so Beverly threw in her full support. Odell told Bishop Brooks that he could make happen his theories from the thesis, and the rest is history.

He passed his thesis defense, and soon thereafter was ordained a reverend. And within a year, Odell's idea became a very real 501(c)(3) nonprofit organization: the Welfare Reform Liaison Project.

CHAPTER 2

Pracademics

Part of pracademics is turning the classroom and agency into a laboratory where students, instructors, and agency personnel participate in real-life program development activities together. Everyone learns. This chapter is about pracademics and how Odell and myself, his agency, and the university became pracademics partners. The chapter shows some details of how we evolved as community and university partners.

THE CLASSROOM

Each time I teach my grant-writing course, I invite agency directors to my class to present an idea that their agency wants to evolve into a program. For those days, I divide the class into five development teams of four members each. After the agency directors present their ideas to the whole class, a speed-dating-like process begins. Directors move to different groups to talk more specifically about their agency and ideas. Students quiz them about program needs and logistics. The students ultimately choose to partner with a director with whom they will eventually develop a program and write a grant—the agencies use the students' proposals to obtain the grant. But first they do extensive research to lay the groundwork for a workable and fundable program.

The agency is promised a thoughtful, well-researched, faculty-guided project. The students, meanwhile, have the opportunity to immerse themselves in a purposeful venture related to their interests, thereby gaining theoretical and operational skills along the way and gaining agency-guided experience. Some have been employed directly as a result of the class.

Over the years, many of Greensboro's agencies have developed sustainable programs through this incubation process. One of those agencies is the Welfare Reform Liaison Project. Six years ago, Odell paired with a team from my class because he knew that the students would do rigorous research and development. Odell presented them with an idea for what I then considered a pie-in-the-sky project to train low-income students in a new dimension of his program: learning digital media production skills. The program today is self-sustaining; it earns enough revenue from the production of its DVDs that students produce for governmental and nonprofit agencies to pay them stipends while they receive practical training. The program has grown to include another section, which trains students to work as employees of firms that transform written records into digital files. Odell's agency is not just producing a ground-floor labor force in digital record keeping; it is shaping a future for those who need a second chance. As has happened on several previous occasions, I didn't quite get where Odell was going with this idea when he presented it to the class, but I said nothing. I have learned over the years not to question Odell's ideas but instead to trust him and focus on how he will implement them.

Odell is the originator, and I am the pragmatist. He may be a bit farsighted, and I may be equally nearsighted, but over time, as we started to see each other's point of view, our bifocals helped put the overall picture into focus.

That things would turn out this way was hardly clear when Odell first came to me with the idea. At the time, I was pretty sure that his vision for a program to help women and their families get off welfare and into the workforce would not make him much money. He had vision, but he had neither a community support strategy nor a program implementation plan.

THE SEEDS OF TRUST SPROUTED OVER A CAESAR SALAD

I decided to enter legitimately into this awkward partnership in 1997 during lunch at a prominent Greensboro steakhouse. Odell was in his business suit, and the whole ordeal had the feel of a high-stakes business lunch, something a social work faculty member doesn't experience too often. It is still Odell's style. He was selling an idea and looking for my personal support and "research-based views." So, there we were, no contracts, no memoranda of agreements, nothing formal—and there still isn't between us. Just a simple "I will help out" on my part.

Dr. Telly Whitfield, a public administrator in northern Virginia, undertook a dissertation research project on how public agencies develop new partnerships with faith-based organizations across Virginia through the formal contracting process. When he found that there were far fewer contractual relationships, but many partnerships, he had to revise his study to show how the numerous informal and some formal partnerships really function at the grassroots level, as they capture an essential dimension of program development at the deepest grass roots. His dissertation's title embodies what he learned in his study: "Handshakes and Hugs: A Study of the Approaches Used by Local Social Service Agencies to Partner with Faith-Based Organizations in Virginia."

Dr. Whitfield's work empirically validates what successful agency leaders know and do but probably never took a test or wrote a paper about. They know that they legitimize their institutional efforts through the glue of service development: what takes place at the numerous breakfast meetings, brown-bag lunch gatherings, chats at school plays or soccer games. People partner with people first, and thus connections have to be made, developed, nurtured, and sustained. People bring their institutional affiliations, which at first may be seemingly unrelated, and eventually tie them into the personal bonds based on the trust built through their personal bonds. In our story, Odell was one of the top sales people in his transportation logistic firm before he ventured on this social service journey into the community, and he was employing his sales strategy with me at lunch.

Salespeople are taught to sell themselves, sell their company, sell their product, and sell their price. Odell sold himself that day, and it was enough for me. Eventually, I twisted that maxim ever so slightly for Odell. He had to sell himself, sell his new agency, sell his programs, and develop a fair and honest budget for the money to start flowing. Odell sold himself at lunch. He was without a real program and had no budget, he was committed to a tough-love approach that didn't sit right with me, and he was in a hurry. But he was passionate, kind, and committed—and what an effort he made, an elegant restaurant, dressed in dapper fashion. He was serious, and he had a dream.

Neither of us remembers whether Odell asked directly for my support. I saw at lunch that his locker-room passion for his new effort was genuine, despite the tough-love path he was choosing to help people chase demons away—their inner fears that hold them back from giving 100 percent in an effort to take a different path from the one they are on—and make the transition from welfare to work. The program also helps them understand and successfully negotiate external barriers like meeting the probation officer's guidelines every time, passing a random drug test, paying child support on time, and doing the things to get and keep a job. The rise of Odell's mother from poverty was phenomenal, but his one-size-fits-all model underscoring a training approach to the variety of women from various circumstances just didn't sit well with me, nor did Odell's rush to get his program under way.

But there was more to what was a simple but profound vision. Sure, Odell was going to take what he learned from his mother's faith, hard work, and never-quit attitude and imbue students in his program with the same gritty spirit and determination he saw in his mother's overcoming of hardship. And he was going to succeed, as is evidenced by the graduation speech of Angelia Ijames—a quiet, humble, unemployed single mom who initially came to the program seeking to better her chances of employment through learning computer skills—at the first graduation ceremony of the Welfare Reform Liaison Project. Angelia initially had been an intern for thirty days at the United Way of Greater Greensboro, where she received a stipend from the Welfare Reform Liaison Project. After a successful trial period, United Way hired her full-time. After that five-year stint, Odell lured Angelia back to his agency to direct community outreach, which she does each day with a perpetual smile. In her speech, Angelia said: "When I came to the Welfare Reform Liaison Project over one year ago, I came looking only to get some computer skills—what I received was a second chance. . . . The compassion, respect, honor, uplifting kind words of encouragement and support I was shown provided me with a foundation to build upon. . . . Reverend Cleveland is always straightforward and bold with the Truth. His sharing of his own life experiences and struggles renewed my hope for tomorrow" (for the full text of Angelia's speech, see appendix 2).

SOMETHING BRAND NEW

Odell was not only going to help chase demons away as he did with Angelia; his program would also prepare students in the program to understand and learn to play by the rules that make the engines of business in America run smoothly. And he would do what no welfare department could do: use his connections in the business community to place his trainees in jobs with supervision by his own small staff, which he didn't have at the time, and share the related expenses with firms until each employee proved worthy of full-time employment. The program was based on the sheltered workshop model in which job-training coaches learn a prospective employee's job and help the firm if the new hire gets sick, has trouble with assignments, or needs other types of support. The roads to hell and doomed program development are paved with good intentions and bad planning. As Odell and I have both learned from sports, the devil is not in the details. It's more like God is in the details, in the little things that are taught during hours of practice.

Planning is about eliminating as much randomness as possible. The material for good human services practice and leadership was inside Odell, but it needed reformatting so that he could understand nonprofit organizations and their similarities and differences from his business format. The people skills and social wisdom were in place. Odell loves to teach and preach, and he can hypnotize a room full of people and have them swimming in their tears by the end. I felt that if Odell could harness those people skills to planning skills, the Welfare Reform Liaison Project could be bigger than life, just like him. Odell had to look before he leaped into the program and community development aspects of his work, which he had learned so well in basketball and in the business world. Now he had to leap hard and fast when the time was right.

At our lunch, Odell told me about how he wanted to start the program before he had the necessary systems in place to underscore successful program development. The best athletes see the whole game even while they play their particular position. I was helping Odell see the whole game of nonprofit development and his position in it. As I listened to Odell's lunchtime game strategy for developing his vision into a program, I watched him eat his steak sandwich while I ate my chicken

Caesar salad, thinking, "Wow! This guy is really passionate, but he will lose the second he steps on the court of human services in Greensboro because he's too quick."

Odell was not very familiar with the details of welfare policy and implementation, and he was aghast when he learned that a welfare recipient with two children made less than $400 a month in North Carolina. He muttered, "I spend more than that on a Friday evening at dinner with a prospective client." At that moment, I thought to myself, "I think I want in with this guy—he's getting it." But the explosions that often go off in the pragmatist's head then went off in my head: "He needs to embody his ideas into a nonprofit organization, who is going to do that? He needs a governance structure—who's going to assemble that group? He needs short-term and long-term financial support—how is he going to get that? He needs partnerships and lots of them—who is going to do that?"

Odell had a vision and passion, he had the institutional support of Mount Zion, he had an idea of what he wanted to do, and latent program development skills. Fortunately, he had none of the doomsday mentality that laces the everyday narrative of the local service system, but he also had no game plan—none of the hours of thinking, testing, and retesting strategies that go into a Saturday afternoon college basketball game. Beyond enthusiasm and the lack of a can't-be-done attitude and the foot-dragging that goes with the attitude, he actually had something new— a business idea that could work in human services—to go along with his passion.

The social services culture embodied in large welfare bureaucracies was moving into workforce development—not by choice but by mandate. Public policy was mandating that welfare bureaucracies fly into workforce development too quickly—but welfare bureaucracies are like penguins; they don't fly. There was simply no way Greensboro's social service bureaucracy would soar into workforce development successfully. One might call ex–welfare recipients customers and ex-caseworkers job developers, but the welfare establishment lacked the quickness that the new policy demanded, and it was too used to controlling its fiefdom. Welfare bureaucracies were closed systems in which the bureaucracies ruled and clients complied. Public welfare agencies had to enter partnerships with rules different from those that had sustained their welfare operations for years. Plus, at the dawning of the Bush era, with the push for faith-based involvement in welfare support services, public welfare agencies, hard pressed to find partners to employ the hard to employ, were reaching in the direction of faith-based agencies for any kind of support. But this was new, and welfare agencies didn't know how to partner equally with the business community or the faith community. Odell almost had everything in place to do both. Odell had connections in the business community, knew its culture, knew what it took to climb the career ladder, and could relate to the deep struggles of his prospective students. He had the core of something that might serve as a prototype for what I call the backside of economic development: training the hardest people to train and employ, people whose past circumstances had made them lose confidence in themselves, which the welfare system made minimal efforts to change. His skills were not part of the institutional life of departments of social services nationally, and certainly not locally.

Odell needed to do some hand shaking and some hugging, much like politicians on the campaign stump, to get the backing he needed to enter successfully into the competition of workforce development; and he had to do so quickly but under control. We spent the rest of 1997 learning more about each other and developing a game plan to launch this new organization. Many things had to be accomplished quickly but prudently. First on the agenda was for the church to downsize its Emergency Assistance Program by creating a nonprofit that would incorporate the program Odell had told Bishop Brooks about. That was a two-step process, handled by lawyers from Mount Zion Baptist Church. On April 28, 1998, Welfare Reform Liaison Project became its own separate nonprofit corporation, a 501(c)(3).

The Welfare Reform Liaison Project had to incorporate in the state of North Carolina and file an application with the IRS to become a 501(c)(3). In doing that, Odell and Bishop Brooks put together a board of directors who would not just form the organization's governing structure but also hire Odell as the organization's new director. The new board would also help plan and shape initiatives, and it would be the legal fiscal agent, separate from the church. The organization had entered the community square—it was no longer part of the church—and it would compete like every other organization for the scarce funding that plagues all human services agencies. Odell would learn that the competition in that arena is fierce.

The gestation of the Welfare Reform Liaison Project could not have come at a better time politically. The Personal Responsibility and Work Opportunity Reconciliation Act of 1996 (aka "welfare reform") had come about during Bill Clinton's presidency, but the final legislation was spawned during the 1994 Republican takeover of the House and Senate in the midterm elections. A puritanical moral narrative, shaped by the religious right, dominated the social narrative and corresponding legislation for the following ten years of Republican-dominated national legislative and eventually executive leadership, and part of it took form in Newt Gingrich's "Contract with America": "THE PERSONAL RESPONSIBILITY ACT: Discourage illegitimacy and teen pregnancy by prohibiting Welfare to minor mothers and denying increased [Aid to Families with Dependent Children] for additional children while on Welfare, cut spending for Welfare programs, and enact a tough two-years-and-out provision with work requirements to promote individual responsibility."

There has been plenty written on this or that aspect of welfare reform from the left, right, and middle, and much written about the problems with its implementation (including by me, in a 2001 book titled *A Limited Partnership: The Politics of*

Religion, Welfare and Social Service). From the right, one gets the impression that Aid to Families with Dependent Children, the program that the Personal Responsibility and Work Opportunity Reconciliation Act of 1996 (PRWORA) replaced, was a long-overdue, essentially tough-love elixir to a policy and practices that discouraged work, promoted laziness, produced poor parenting role models, was a major contributor to teen pregnancy, and ultimately was the central explanation for poverty. The law's short title, Temporary Assistance for Needy Families (TANF), linguistically and in reality, demonstrated that the entitlement was subsidiary. People could get government help, but it would be temporary and they would have to help themselves, seek out community support, and go to work, jobs or not.

The right characterized the typical welfare recipient as a black woman with several aliases that she used to secure as many welfare checks as possible. She drove a big Cadillac, with a slew of kids in the backseat. She did this, of course, at the expense of hardworking taxpayers. The liberal critique, as usual, was a bit more nuanced. It agreed with some of the increasingly dominant right-wing analyses, with a string of caveats that ends, however, making the right seem wrong. While the theorists on the left and right were shadowboxing, the locals had to fight the ravages of people scared to death. They were hungry, some slept in cars, some doubled and tripled up with family or friends, and their kids still had to go to school. These were the hard facts that left and right theorists didn't have to deal with. Odell and the community did. The theorists would note that, yes, between 15 percent and 20 percent of welfare recipients had received benefits for more than five years and shared some of the characteristics embedded in the stereotypes. They argued, however, that the average recipient had received benefits for eighteen or fewer months, that she was likely to be the last hired and first fired (and thus bounced on and off welfare), that she was a single parent with less than two children. To dull the right-wing critique, liberals would note that there were just as many whites receiving public assistance as blacks, knowing full well that proportion of the population is the accurate measure. (In a population of 100, if ninety people are white and ten are black, and 10 percent of the population is on welfare, then all else being equal, nine white people and one black person would be on welfare—but statistics were showing that six were white and four were black. In reality, it was 51 percent white to 49 percent black, so saying more whites than blacks are on welfare is correct but politically motivated.) However, even though whites vastly outnumber blacks on welfare, the number of whites on welfare with regard to their number in the population was far less than blacks. The liberal narrative went on to talk about the stable floor that welfare provided for children with a mom present in the home and how cruel and unjust it was for a policy to make poor women and children negotiate a dynamic and competitive marketplace without a government safety net.

What has become the norm in American politics has far less to do with developing policies whose programs actually work on the ground than with creating the narrative that unites or wins back the voting public's favor and thus consolidates the public's power by eroding the other side's power. Conservatives and liberals create narratives to kill each other's ideas—often at the expense of sober program implementation. But the power grab in shaping the actual implementation of a policy supposedly directed toward changing behaviors and social outcomes can also seem logical from afar but have nothing to do with reality: training, transportation, child care, job placement, retention, and outcomes.

The current of welfare policy in Washington during the 1990s was moving fast, driven by quite a bit of hot air, from the ground up, but the cold reality in North Carolina was that the policy was kicking in just at the time that textile and furniture manufacturing jobs were drifting, and later speeding, toward China. Tobacco-related jobs were disappearing as well. Before 2003, it had been during the Great Depression that so many people had been thrown out of work at one time in North Carolina. An e-mail to the Greensboro Displaced Worker Committee, of which Odell was a member, from the director of the Department of Social Services in Greensboro noted that many of the traditional safety-net programs did not meet the needs of displaced workers, whose needs vary greatly—both in extent and in timing for training in new industries. "We need a very flexible response system to meet them where they are. We need to work closely with the private sector to be able to anticipate surges in demand and changing needs."

The crisis throughout the South was not just about people's character, sexual behavior (according to the right wing), and the like. It has been about what the loss of jobs means to families and how communities must reconfigure their services to meet the aftermath of economic disaster at the personal, family, and community levels. The members of the Displaced Worker Committee were the top leaders in Greensboro's social service and economic development systems: Social Services, the United Way, the Urban Ministry, the Chamber of Commerce, the Worker Investment Council, Odell's Welfare Reform Liaison Project, and a major community foundation, the Joseph M. Bryan Foundation. These were local leaders who knew that moving people "from welfare to work" or calling those who had turned to welfare after being laid off customers, as our local Department of Social Services had done, was little more than a cute saying—the economic current was moving out to sea. This economic shift in North Carolina happened more slowly in the 1990s than it did during the recession of the early part of the following decade, but it was a trend, and leaders here knew it. Odell had seen it coming, as had other economic and civic leaders, but Odell and others had to do what they could with what they had until they could invent the future. The economic shift to China occurred despite a narrative that was winning political power. People on the ground are just too overwhelmed trying to survive to put policy making and power grabbing as their main priority. To understand why Odell was invited to the table in 2003 with prominent leaders in social services and workforce and economic development, people who would make decisions about our region, it is essential to understand not only where the Welfare Reform Liaison Project was in 1998 but also where it was heading and how it would get there.

The Welfare Reform Liaison Project got its name because it was going to be a broker that used community resources, especially the business community, as an essential part of helping women, and initially a man or two, get employed and stay employed despite the shifting economic current. It would train people and monitor their progress while providing support to its students and to employers who took the risk of hiring "the unemployable." It was quite a task for a new agency in tough economic times and in the midst of a dramatic policy change.

The social and political narrative at the time of the Welfare Reform Liaison Project's birth hit Odell and me hard and differently. The focus of the narrative was an interesting blend of blacks being immoral and a social policy that enabled increased immorality because government had been, for too long, rewarding slothfulness and wild sexual behavior. The inaccuracy of these claims about the causes of welfare, which came from both left and right, as well as statistical analyses of the effects of the policy nationally, are well documented elsewhere. In our experience, though, North Carolina was losing its manufacturing base and the Piedmont Triad, the central part of North Carolina, was a manufacturing hub for textiles and furniture. Our truth was that welfare reform had kicked in during overall good economic times of the late 1990s but in increasingly eroding economic times in North Carolina. The local system of services was not ready for the concrete and objective changes of the new welfare laws. As we all saw with Hurricane Katrina, when a disaster hits and a community is not prepared, all hell breaks loose. Welfare reform was not Katrina, but it was a disaster.

Of course, Odell and I spent much time arguing from our personal and academic perches about the new laws and how he would develop his organization in response to the national narrative and the local reality, which were working at cross-purposes. But there were truths in both political narratives—but not all the truth, as each side would like everyone to believe.

Odell grew up and had lived in the midst of a welfare culture—he saw how some people on welfare abused the system, how fathers were absent, and how absenteeism ruined young men especially. Eventually, he would look into the eyes of men who, like Odell, had absentee fathers and challenge them to be real men and take responsibility for their children. He was changing a narrative one black man at a time, and I have seen him do it. But he would also sit at the table with business, economic, public, and nonprofit leaders to try to create a new economic future for the region. Odell's brain cells were synthesizing an organizational strategy in which he would become a potent one-on-one force and a powerful leader in the community.

Odell preached to me that faith and hard work could make a difference in helping people turn away from the welfare culture. He made clear that I was the theorist and he was the practitioner who saw more than grains of truth in the right-wing narrative, and he sounded too right wing for me. Our views of the complex intersection of government and private responsibility might be best characterized this way: I am an old-fashioned liberal who believes that if someone is stuck twenty feet offshore, government should throw a thirteen-foot rope and say, "Swim—we have met you more than halfway." Odell is more conservative, and his government would throw a ten-foot rope—he believes in a hand up, not a handout. I lectured at Odell, called him Jerry Falwell, and asked him over and over, "If morality underpins hard work, why doesn't the right wing go after corporate welfare cheats?" And on we have gone until this day, each moving ever gradually toward understanding the other's view of welfare. Odell's increasing involvement with people in the community who were concerned with broader economic development and my attending the classes he taught on personal growth and development truly brought to each of us a deeper understanding of the other's view.

CHAPTER 3

A Faith-Based Nonprofit
Buries Research in a Program Grant

New agencies, especially faith-based nonprofits, rarely start out with solid research and development. Doing so is not so simple. Funders don't fund research that often, and new agencies don't start out by thinking about research—but it should be that way. The Welfare Reform Liaison Project received its first grant for research. This chapter shows the hurdles we overcame to win our first community grant and thus start our program with solid research. The intended by-product of the research was that Odell was able to use it to do some old-fashioned community organizing.

WHAT IS A REQUEST FOR PROPOSALS?

The same day the Welfare Reform Liaison Project received notification of its nonprofit status, the first of many financial opportunities came our way. Bishop Brooks handed Odell a request for proposals (RFP) from the United Way of Greater Greensboro's Bryan Foundation Grant Program.

The RFP was much like RFPs from local funders across the country. The grant committee was interested in proposals for a $25,000 grant that would address the following issues: (1) obstacles that prevent people from achieving self-sufficiency, such as transportation or child care; (2) issues that are a direct cause of other problems, such as substance abuse or lack of parenting skills; and (3) issues that inhibit service effectiveness, such as system fragmentation or lack of focus on prevention.

The deadline for submitting the RFP was May 29, 1998, at five in the afternoon. The Post-it note attached to the copy that landed on my desk was dated May 1—just twenty-eight days before the deadline: "Bob, Pastor Brooks gave me this info today. Please advise, Odell."

There was an entire book in that Post-it note, and Odell had received a clear message from his boss that he had better produce. He had no idea what was in between the lines of what Bishop Brooks had handed him. If the RFP had been from his prior employer to get a contract from a new customer, Odell would have known exactly what to do, and he would have noticed all the subtleties being cast his way—there would be little said and little needing to be said. But his situation had changed. He was a new minister (not yet ordained), had taken a $20,000 pay cut, had lost the company car and his expense account. For Odell, developing a program was exciting, scary, and bewildering at the same time.

Bishop Brooks had the authority to ordain Odell—and he was sending him a loud and clear message that the church was going to be a hand up for Odell, not a handout. Mount Zion's community ministry was a new nonprofit, and for the nonprofit to be effective, it had to become self-sustaining. And to become self-sustaining, Bishop Brooks was making it clear that Odell had better get to work immediately and get some money.

In Bishop Brooks's playbook, luck doesn't get money; hard work does. Odell really didn't know how to get money for human services projects. Today he is the master of doing so, but all masters had to take their first steps. Bishop Brooks, a patient man, knew what his church would face with the welfare changes that would take effect locally in August 1998. The bishop is a successful leader inside and outside of his congregation, and he expects as much from members of his leadership circle inside and outside the church. Odell had to move not just for the women and children he proposed to help but also for his own standing in an extremely reputable community church. In the abstract, Odell understood clearly that if he did not make the program sustainable, he would be fired. However, he did not know how to get funding in the community. In between the lines of the RFP was a message to Odell to go get external funding.

From the beginning, Bishop Brooks knew I was helping Odell. I had conducted the board's first retreat at the church and used the opportunity to hold my social work administration class in conjunction with the retreat. That kind of community-engaged teaching in a practice setting had a double impact. I don't know how comfortable the students were with the setting, especially the white ones—for many of them it was their first time in a black church—since the retreat took place in Mount Zion's sanctuary. Every church event inside the church begins with blessings and prayers—it feels religious because it is.

But Bishop Brooks had let me teach my entire graduate course at Mount Zion without charge, which is not the case when universities or other community groups that can afford to pay want to use the church's classrooms over the long term. I believe Bishop Brooks assumed Odell would have me at his side during the shift from emergency assistance to community player.

We had just four weeks—twenty-eight days—to develop a program plan that met at least two of the three criteria in the United Way RFP and to build a good foundation of trust from the church. He was in pretty deep, and he didn't know it.

More important, the Welfare Reform Liaison Project was still just an internal operation of the church—Odell was on a one-year leash and had to examine ways to build the Emergency Assistance Program into a more community-focused operation that addressed community-wide concerns around welfare. But Odell was still a minister of Mount Zion reporting to his new board about his ministerial functions. On paper, the organization was a separate entity, but in reality, it would be many years before the community saw it and Mount Zion as two separate but nevertheless connected organizations. This is the gray area in between being of the church and from the community.

Up until that moment, the organizational and community work that had taken place had focused on piecing together a board to govern the new nonprofit, working out logistical arrangements with the church to take over the building that housed the former Emergency Assistance Program, figuring out how to compensate Odell over the long haul, and meeting leaders and decision makers in the community who could open doors for him. A study of the Emergency Assistance Program was completed, a board of directors was formed, and a committee structure was in place. I cannot emphasize enough how such steps are often afterthoughts of new nonprofits. From the outset, the Welfare Reform Liaison Project always worked to balance the visible world of program services with the not-so-visible world of strong infrastructure.

A few months before receiving the RFP, I had suggested that Odell make multiple copies of the Welfare Reform Liaison Project's business plan, which in actuality was a conceptual plan to move the Emergency Assistance Program into a training program. The best part of Odell's plan was a colorful graph that counted how much more money Mount Zion had been distributing to the needy over the previous three years than in the five before that. As my college economics teacher drilled into me, "If you can't count it, it doesn't count."

Odell loved his plan, in a little blue book, and absolutely loved shopping it around to key community people to inform them of the new venture and possibly pick up a few board members, which he did. One was a social worker from the Department of Social Services who worked with welfare recipients; another was a community outreach volunteer from the largest white church in Greensboro, the First Presbyterian Church. Bishop Brooks may have innocently given Odell the RFP, as Odell believed, but I truly believed that it was his way of telling Odell to go get some money for this program so it could start to be financially independent of the church.

Bishop Brooks was made an ex officio member of the board of directors, which was an important decision. Odell wanted to make sure there was a firewall between the church and the Welfare Reform Liaison Project. If things went well, great. If not, the church and its more than five thousand members would be protected legally.

However, the church would never really be independent of the Welfare Reform Liaison Project, and the Welfare Reform Liaison Project would never be independent of the church. And yet if the project flopped, then the bishop wasn't a voting member of the board, so the church wasn't liable. We discuss the relationship of the church with Welfare Reform Liaison Project in more detail in later chapters, as it typifies some of the interplay of the community, the black church, and the building of community development corporations, which often but not always are nonprofits that emerge from churches and handle matters from advocacy to economic development, and many things in between, that strengthen low-income communities.

Twenty-eight days to write a small grant proposal is usually no big ordeal for agencies that have boilerplate material that go into proposals and experienced staff to write the narratives. The Welfare Reform Liaison Project had neither—and Odell had no experience whatsoever.

I normally spend sixteen weeks with my students—three hours of class time each week, plus office hours—to answer questions and point to different things that would strengthen the plan in any good proposal. It is slow-motion mentoring—which is how it ought to be for newcomers to the grant-winning game. For the Welfare Reform Liaison Project's first grant, we didn't have sixteen weeks, so we had to have speed under control.

We agreed to frame the grant proposal around two of the three themes: issues that inhibit service effectiveness, such as system fragmentation and lack of prevention focus, and obstacles that prevent people from achieving self-sufficiency, such as transportation or child care.

Our major obstacle with regard to real program development was finding out whether other congregations in the black community were going to take on this issue, because the Welfare Reform Liaison Project would surely sink before it set sail if there wasn't cooperation, and it would not receive support over the long haul if Odell was not known by other clergy and community outreach people from congregations in the black community. Fortunately for us, everyone who had anything to do with the welfare changes—which in one way or another amounted to quite a few people and organizations in the community—threw up their hands crazily in the air, not knowing where else to look for help, except to the black church. We said as much in the grant narrative: "As the new welfare reform takes hold in the Greensboro community, we are going to have to pull all of our resources in order to help people who lose their support from the public system. At this particular time nobody knows what the churches are doing and nobody knows what the churches can do. This is system fragmentation! As people realize that they can no longer go to public agencies, they are going to have to spend an absorbing amount of time and energy (and they may fail) trying to find some immediate help."

The women being pushed off the welfare rolls were scared and desperate and inundating local nonprofits and the emergency assistance efforts of congregations. In the chaos, the community's largest African-American church had an opportunity to act calm and sober and to get a handle on this problem. But the crisis was not calm, and the national narrative was not sober. Everyone at the community level, especially the United Way, knew the chaos to be real, and the national narrative and local chaos affected the grant committee members as much as anyone. There is a large difference between a policy narrative that proclaims it will have contracting provisions for community support, and the very real local problems when ten families show up on a church's steps scared, hungry, and full of fears about paying the bills and taking care of their children's needs.

IMPORTANCE OF DATA ON THE BLACK CHURCHES IN GREENSBORO

For all his vision, Odell was going to sink if he didn't know who was doing what in the black churches in Greensboro and if he couldn't explain how his efforts could be supportive and not duplicative to the white funding community. The theme of the RFP was to eliminate the fragmentation caused by the realities of the policy changes and to do so by bringing together various members of the religious community to support Odell's new project by connecting their efforts with Odell's and his with theirs. This is how we worded it in the proposal:

> Welfare Reform Liaison Project is going to bring together the fragmented pieces of services in the faith community and broker information about all of those services. This project will assess what the faith community is doing and what it is capable of doing. In the next several years, as welfare reform eliminates people from the roles (whether they have jobs or not) we will hear more requests for help at Mount Zion, and throughout the white and black faith community. Mount Zion and most others are not prepared for the expected increased demands for emergency assistance.

We had to do some acrobatics in the section of the grant proposal that asked us to address specific needs. We had to write the proposal in such a way that the grant allocation committee would approve funding for a program we didn't yet have fully up and running. That would've been hard enough by itself, but what we were really trying to get the money for was research and to bring the community together, and that made the task even more difficult. We employed the economic maxim we previously mentioned about counting:

The specific need that is being addressed is this: where are the women and children who are no longer eligible for Work First (North Carolina's term for the new public effort) going to get help when they are hungry, they don't have any clothes, they don't have a place to stay when traditional places like Urban Ministry are full, and they don't know where to turn? Presently there are 1,009 families in Guilford County receiving TANF monies (welfare benefits). Come August we are going to have our first 29 families who are no longer eligible to receive cash assistance. What will happen to those families? Even if the economy remains strong, by the end of the year 100 people won't have jobs nor be eligible for services—100 mothers and 200 kids. Again we must ask the question: What will happen to these families?

We had to write a proposal that accomplished many goals. Odell, who loved talking to people, had to sell his program in the black community. He loved that idea. But to know who was doing what, and to prove it if called on to do so, he needed more than a few anecdotes. To complicate matters, he needed a salary from outside of Mount Zion. The Welfare Reform Liaison Project was its own program, and it would have to be self-supporting sooner rather than later because the church was not paying Odell much. Winning a grant would indicate that Odell could get onto the road of self-sufficiency in the one year Bishop Brooks had given him to make his program work.

For planning purposes, we needed proof for the funding community that the program wasn't stepping on the toes of other, more established programs. So Odell would conduct a needs assessment, but the framing for funders could not have a whiff of university-backed research in it. He also had to make sure that his narrative was about filling a gap in fragmented services by bringing congregations together to help women in particular transition from years on welfare to sustainable work. So in the proposal we gave a picture of his program as follows:

Welfare Reform Liaison Project is ultimately going to provide service to women by teaching them basic skills GED classes, budgeting, decision making, stress management and help with financial resources. We will also help women connect with other resources and people in the community and churches that will provide services such as child care, transportation, training, access to job networks, and coordination with other agencies.

We brought the two aspects of the program together in one sentence: "We cannot succeed without knowing who is doing what in the faith community." A quick example might be helpful here. Because no one was offering training for welfare recipients in the church or nonprofit sector, we knew that if we won this grant and then others to start the program, we would have a resource bank of churches in the black community that could help us provide support in things such as child care, to make the segue into work easier. The research was the easiest way for us to get the most reliable information to help in program development.

I had no time to write the first draft of the proposal, although I was deeply involved in reconstructing the next three drafts. So I told Odell to respond to the specific issues raised in the application—system fragmentation, specific need, specific population served, activities and timetable, and budget—and get it back to me in three days. This would give us time to revise and plan out the other essential things that had to be in this grant, like getting letters of support from different agency leaders and Bishop Brooks which usually meant making personal visits that take time. We had to be together, and we both had different schedules, so there was quite a bit going on in a short period of time to teach a new grant writer how the process worked. But Odell's earlier informational meetings with local key players paid off as he convinced community big shots to write letters of support. Our three-day deadline for the first draft would give us time to rewrite and go over the narrative that he was likely to present at the informational meeting he would attend on May 7 for prospective applicants.

I critiqued Odell's first draft of the proposal no differently than the way I mark up my student's proposals in class. I scrutinize every word, and the first draft ends up looking like a bloody nose with red all over the place. Odell was stunned—mad as can be, to put it mildly—but he saw it like the "suicide" sprinting drills that basketball coaches put their players through to get them in shape for a long season of grueling competition. His tail tucked between his legs, he said he knew that he would get stronger, much like he knew years later that the students from my class who had no experience in grant writing would get stronger by the time they had completed the course. He grinned and bore the embarrassment of that first pregame attempt to prepare to earn community money.

PRESENTING TO FUNDING COMMITTEE

When Odell walked into the informational session at the United Way on May 7, 1998, he was prepared to speak clearly about what he wanted to accomplish. We had written two drafts and prepared the final proposal before that meeting, and he was ready to explain how connecting with local clergy would prevent further fragmentation in the confused system that newly minted welfare dropouts were besieging. And he could talk cogently about his program-to-be and connect the two community needs to his project, which the United Way was giving away funds to address.

A slight smile comes to Odell's face when he reflects back on walking into the United Way for the grant orientation session. As a man steeped in the business culture, it was very interesting for him to walk into a building and be directed into a large room full of "mostly white folks" and not a soul other than him wearing a suit. Today you still won't find Odell at any community meeting without a suit and without being extremely prepared. He is all business.

The orientation session started with everyone going around the room to introduce themselves and the agency they were representing. When it was his turn, he said in a nervous voice, "My name is Minister Odell Cleveland and I am the President of Welfare Reform Liaison Project Inc., a faith-based nonprofit organization out of Mount Zion Baptist Church."

The United Way staff person who was running the session stopped and said, "What did you say?" So Odell repeated himself. As he recalled afterward, "She looked at me as if to say, 'Another church group after money.'" Later in the orientation, she made the point loudly and clearly that the United Way "did not fund churches."

We made it clear in the grant proposal that the Welfare Reform Liaison Project was from the church but was not the church itself, a nuance that would both help us and hound us over the years.

Odell later found out that the woman who was conducting the session was a member of Evangel Fellowship Church, another black church in Greensboro that had developed a nonprofit spinoff from its congregation. And as it happens, one of the nonprofit organizations in the room was a group called Malachi House, which was developed under the leadership of Evangel's senior pastor, Otis Locket. It was being run by an elder of that church named Cliff Lovick, who was being paid by the church and who had received previous grants from the United Way of Greater Greensboro. Fortunately, Lovick's program was for substance abuse prevention, and substance abuse services are easier to fund than system fragmentation.

Odell was a businessman turned minister and a new nonprofit director. He had heard many of my minilectures on the realities of local social service politics, especially around money. But to understand the trust that developed over the years between the two of us is to understand that Odell is a visual and experiential learner. Once he began to see and experience what I was lecturing about, he would incorporate the ideas into his operational strategy in the community.

"Eliminating system fragmentation was about building common unity," Odell said years later. "Three things the young lady didn't understand were that I was prepared for this meeting, we were a real 501(c)(3), and I played to win."

We went on to write the grant about system fragmentation and how we needed to prevent folks from falling for the third and fourth time into the cracks in the social service delivery system. We used Mount Zion's legitimacy as a successful community servant as part of the grant narrative and agency history, as we still didn't have a program. We said as much in the grant proposal's cover letter: "The Welfare

Reform Liaison Project is a new nonprofit organization housed at Mount Zion Baptist Church."

On the surface, the proposal addressed system fragmentation, but we needed a way to drive home the fact that real people were suffering, that there was a serious need to figure out who could help in the religious and social service community, and that this new organization had the skills to find out who was helping and bring them together for collective action.

INTANGIBLES IN THE GRANT GAME

I chaired the local United Way's grant committee in the 1980s. It was the same as the committee that was going to review Odell's proposal but now had different members. In my two years as chair of the committee, community volunteers read more than fifty proposals. If there was one theme that ran through 90 percent of the proposals that caused the people who were not social service experts on the committee the greatest consternation, it was how people soliciting funds talked more about how their programming efforts would plug the gaps in the service delivery system than about how, in concrete terms, they would help the people they were serving. For a scholar like myself used to social service speak, such language was no problem, but the insider's narrative irritated the reviewers to no end.

At one meeting, an accountant for a major corporation came into the conference room of the United Way, dropped his stack of twenty proposals on the table, and declared in disgust that none of the proposals should be funded. At the end of a day of reading and reviewing proposals, the reader, professional or volunteer alike, should be hooked by the energy, passion, and urgency in a request for funds. A new organization or an organization trying something new must teach grant proposal readers who they are and what they will accomplish with and on behalf of those people they serve—and it must do so confidently.

Other things count as well, like the track record of the organization, the strength of its governing board, and its reputation in the broader community. But the newer the agency, the more important it is that it explain a well-planned effort in an understandable and heartfelt way. Reviewers do not judge a new organization in the same way that they judge the Salvation Army or the Red Cross, plain and simple. If and when the prospective grantee gets an audience with the funder, energy, passion, and urgency should scent the meeting. So our proposal had to express something positive to readers, even though we were talking about something as boring as system fragmentation—clearly an insider's euphemism for a group of agencies trying to solve, manage, or prevent the same problem, but like playing pin-the-tail-on-the-donkey instead of trying to hit the target with the blindfold removed.

In my grant-writing class, there's a particular exercise I always give my students. I instruct them as follows: "You come home from a long day at work only to find that your upstairs and downstairs toilets have overflowed. Please draw a picture of the problem as if you are presenting it to a funder who funds these problems."

No words are allowed in the drawing. I then ask them individually to get up in front of the class to explain their problem to the class. Toilets, running water, wet furniture, and the like invariably dominate 85 percent of the pictures. There are rarely people in the picture, and if so, they are an afterthought. All the explanations are about fixing the toilet.

We laugh and joke until the last presenter, and then I "gong" them (a gong has been a fixture in my classroom for years). I go on to tell them that none would get funding because of the way they presented the problem. There are no such things as toilets without people. The overflow is causing a problem for people. The picture has to be people-dominated.

Yes, they would be writing grants about gaps in services, weak links in the supply chain of local services, or replumbing outdated communication lines within and across service sectors with web development and blogs. But to funders and grant review committees, all of that plumbing means nothing if they don't feel a strong connection to how fixing something in service provision affects people and how the proposed solution will make their lives better. I tell my students that when they write their narratives about services, they have to take a backseat to people. (As creative expressions of thanks, one class gave me a signed toilet seat when the course ended, and another gave me a whole commode sprayed in colorful stucco.)

Odell and I used the chaos in the system as another way to say calmly that the new program could reduce confusion by serving women and their families, by helping people in Greensboro attain financial stability. Odell overwhelmed the committee by vowing to go and talk to half of the 161 pastors in the black community—which he did—to find out how to connect them to our efforts and us to theirs. Our lazy Susan was born in that grant—the entire set of building blocks of Welfare Reform Liaison Project, including the faith summit.

In August 1998, Odell got word that we had won $25,000. Shortly after the Welfare Reform Liaison Project received the money, Bishop Brooks ordained Odell, who from that day onward was officially Reverend Calvin Odell Cleveland.

We both learned so much from Odell's interviews with members of the black faith community that I suggested the Welfare Reform Liaison Project hold a summit to present the findings to the community, which is labeled a "community meeting" in the grant-making world. Odell thought it was a great idea, and he came up with the idea of a faith summit.

Since then, the Welfare Reform Liaison Project has held a faith summit every second year, attracting more than five hundred people from across the region each time to network and connect program ideas in both the faith-based and the secular service systems.

Ironically enough, the United Way of Greater Greensboro became a cosponsor of the faith summit and took as much credit as it could for reaching out to the black community. The United Way later wanted the Welfare Reform Liaison Project to become a member agency, but Odell declined its invitation to join, a decision that we discuss in greater detail in a later chapter. Nevertheless, Odell is now on the United Way's board of directors.

Throughout the rest of the book, we refer to this specific grant as the smoke-and-mirrors grant because we had to perform a bit of conceptual magic to earn the grant. As pracademics, we looked at the process knowing that the readers would be citizen volunteers and that the staff of the United Way would go over the grant with a fine-toothed comb. Being a venture grant, we also knew that there was a chance that if a well-written, thoughtful, practical research grant made it through the committee, it may just get funded, and with Mount Zion's backing, we thought they would see the venture as legitimate. Even today, it is hard to believe that a new agency like the Welfare Reform Liaison Project convinced a mainline funder to take a venture-capital-like risk before it had a program in place. The United Way committee took the risk and funded the project, and there was a huge return—$100 million on the initial investment, in the value of the products that came through the distribution center, salaries, volunteer time, grants, and other in-kind services. And we can't evaluate the savings society has received by keeping people out of jail, putting welfare recipients to work, having more stable homes for the children of our students, and making payments of child support to the families of kids who would have otherwise gone without.

In the next era of human service development—when I hope more community agencies team up with engaged scholars—funders will no longer argue that they don't fund research because it takes away from direct services. The Welfare Reform Liaison Project started out using Odell's data collection to launch its community connections, something that continues today. But back in 1997, we had to bury the research in smoke and mirrors—something no biotech, energy, or pharmaceutical company would ever consider doing, or, for that matter, any sane business with long-term goals.

CHAPTER 4

Bessie the Cow—Let's Do Lunch

This chapter moves a bit off the chronological timeline to illustrate how pracademics works in the daily life of an academic and an agency activist while showing how regular events for an agency in the community are intricately tied to both its past and its future through economic development. By bringing in the present, we thought we could demonstrate the connections to the past and the future. We emphasize how important it is to use the right language at the right time. We have always fought over this, and we still do, but now we listen to each other very carefully.

USE OF RELIGIOUS LANGUAGE

One of the major problems Odell and I had early on was that he used religious language anywhere and everywhere. When Odell became a minister, he was rightfully proud, and he talked like a minister regardless of who he was talking to.

I talked to him, argued with him, pleaded with him to speak the language of those he was speaking to. It would be awfully hard for Odell to widen his sphere of influence in the community if he didn't learn how to be bilingual or trilingual. He would soon come to understand how important language is in shaping a community discussion.

I knew at the time that Odell had to learn to speak to his audience, but as I made clear to him even back then, even I didn't always grasp the importance of speaking the language of my audience. When I was a twenty-one-year-old college student, I had a total inability to understand S. I. Hyakawa's ladder of abstraction, from the field of communication theory, which illustrates gradations of thinking and language from indistinct to specific. I had to study Hyakawa for a test in a communications class, so I went for help to Dr. Willard, a soft-spoken, laid-back, easily approachable elderly professor. I asked him to explain the ladder of abstraction (for a sample, see figure 3).

Dr. Willard saw the blank stare in my eyes as he was explaining the ladder, so he zeroed in on the fourth column—the economy, farm assets, cattle, and Bessie the cow. Suddenly, it all made sense.

Level 4	Society	Human endeavors	Economy
Level 3	Most people	Industries	Farm assets
Level 2	Spoiled child	Cosmetic company	Cattle
Level 1	My sister Tracy	Max Factor Inc.	Bessie the cow

Source: *http://ol.scc.spokane.edu/jstrever/comp/Summer201/hw3.htm.*

FIGURE 3. *Sample Abstraction Ladders*

I understood the complex notion of an economy only vaguely, even though my father's mom-and-pop clothing store was part of the economy. But I understood that the clothes on the racks were the assets—sweaters were big sellers in the cold Northeast where I grew up—and that the blue pullover I was wearing was in the same category as that farmer's Bessie the cow!

Falstaff's line in *Henry IV*, "there are owls and there are larks," took on a new meaning. In a creative and very clear way, in that line, Shakespeare was depicting an aspect of human nature that is today called, rather dully and scientifically, circadian rhythms. When placed on the ladder of abstraction, the two birds suddenly made perfect sense. Subtleties and concreteness of language meant nothing to me until then. Since then, Bessie the cow has gone from being a simple quiz question to a metaphor for one of the guiding principles in social work: meeting clients where they are at.

Odell would eventually appreciate the wisdom of Bessie the cow, but back in those early days, the ladder of abstraction was a foreign concept that he needed to figure out quickly. He had to develop a story line that was equally intelligible to Mr. Mo Sellers, a super volunteer from the "white" First Presbyterian Church, the corporate partners at Wal-Mart headquarters in Arkansas, and Angelia in his personal growth and development class. A key to shaping the narrative in the community about the Welfare Reform Liaison Project rested in Odell's ability to use the ladder of abstraction so that kingmakers and paupers alike would understand him, buy in, and become stakeholders. Whether he was talking about economic changes and their effects on welfare or second chances, his themes had to share a common thread. And Odell had to make on-the-spot decisions about whether his listeners understood him, what to say if they did, and how to know and then adjust if they didn't.

Using only the language of God was simply not enough to successfully shape the story in a multilayered system of services. In our private moments, especially after we hit on the smoke-and-mirrors grant, Odell trusted me enough that I could be candid. I told him that he had to be of the community and from the church—in that order—and that he had to know when and with whom he could and couldn't speak the ministerial language.

We celebrated that first grant, of course. We knew that we had earned it, though we never guessed that it would be followed by more than $100 million in grants, contracts, donated goods, and volunteer hours, not to mention the cost savings to society for putting the difficult to employ to work and to keep them working. Thousands of hours and numerous handshakes and hugs won the Welfare Reform Liaison Project that first grant.

Odell and I played basketball together three days a week, and we knew that both a fade-away jumper and an easy lay-up count for two points, but they're hardly the same shot. The Malachi House, another nonprofit group from a black church competing for the $25,000 United Way grant, shot the easy lay-up. Malachi House was going after something much more tangible than addressing system fragmentation. The organization was seeking money for drug treatment. Malachi House aimed to sober up drug addicts and help change lives—and it had an established reputation, an organization in place, and a staff member of the United Way who went to Evangel, the affiliated church.

Odell, in contrast, was taking a long shot, and the odds were against him. We were both elated that he got money to start the program in earnest. I could show Odell out of the gate how learning both quantitatively and qualitatively about the needs of the community would ground the community development aspect of his agency's evolution with usable information. But Bessie and the ladder of abstraction had to coach us.

I TRUSTED A MINISTER TO BE A SURVEY RESEARCHER: A RISK WORTH TAKING!

Odell was going into a nonprofit world suspicious of surveys and churches, and he consciously had to traverse the ladder of abstraction with every constituency. Everyone had to understand him, all the time.

Odell's first test was convincing dozens of very busy people in Greensboro to give him a few minutes of their valuable time. I knew that to get the Welfare Reform Liaison Project on firm institutional footing, we had to get hard data from the busy people in the agencies and the community members in the trenches.

However, nonprofit leaders have been surveyed to death, and many are understandably hesitant to spend their time on yet another set of questions. Their biggest complaint is that the surveys "never help them," so Odell needed to promise to inform respondents of the results—and he had to deliver on that promise. In my experience, a reputation, good or bad, lasts about five years in a local human services community. The last thing Odell wanted was to make a promise that he could not keep—especially "just" to secure some survey data.

Imagine being a church leader at a time when women were knocking down your door for help. Along comes this new preacher and CEO of a nonprofit wanting your time to respond to a survey. Unless Odell had the right connections with the clergy he was surveying, the clergy would need divine help to make the connections between those real people in need knocking on the door and Odell's survey.

Every move he made in the public square would come back to, or at, Mount Zion—and then him. For Odell's sake, even though the organization was separate from the church, he had to be careful. He had to be more or less from Mount Zion depending on whom he was talking to, but he could never exactly be Mount Zion itself. He had to be about changing welfare to work without maligning the penguins at the Department of Social Services that could not fly (but would still be his flying partners). He was conducting a university-backed survey that I developed to assess congregational service provision and community concerns, but he could not be academic. He had to be able to go up and down the ladder of abstraction easily, quickly, and thoughtfully depending on what kind of person he was engaging with—a white clergy person, a black clergy person, a United Way representative, a young ex-prisoner in his personal development class, or the many other people who Odell interacts with on a daily basis.

We both agreed that Odell had to administer the survey, as we needed as many surveys completed as possible. Odell, being a minister had a better chance of getting in the door to get the survey than an academic researcher. The more surveys completed, the better and more accurate would be the assessment of support services in faith community. A positive by-product of community organization would be that Odell could connect with many religious leaders in the community and learn much from them—and they would learn about the Welfare Reform Liaison Project in terms they could relate to, from Odell, not second- or thirdhand. A minister calling on another minister to solicit information or data is a much easier task than a university researcher or his or her research assistant calling on a clergy member. Clergy speak the same language to each other, and Odell had to translate the survey into gospel. This commonsense principle is no longer just a part of the body of practice wisdom, at least for the scholar who has done the most door-to-door congregational research in the world: Dr. Ram Cnaan of the University of Pennsylvania.

Ram Cnaan and I conducted a thorough research project for the United Way of Delaware to understand how the religious community contributed to the community's social service delivery. We found that intricate and long-term partnerships formed the glue of that community's service delivery system. Strikingly, we found that if an agency had a clergy member on staff, and 34 percent did, then the agency averaged eleven more partnerships with the religious community than did agencies that had no clergy on staff. Clergy, like Odell Cleveland, are pastors without pews, their "pew" is the community.

One might ask whether Cnaan or I used the ministerial strategy to get our data. The answer is that Cnaan has used such a strategy for years in many of his research projects, but I did not for my portion of this collaborative project. In my case, I felt there were other ways to achieve high survey response rates, such as that which I employed in Delaware for my portion of the project. But those methods—follow-up mailings and phone calls—take time, money, and persistence, which there was more of in the Delaware study than what Odell had.

Odell had to work fast because he had to turn his research into a program with outcomes, and he didn't have two years to show the community funders of the United Way of Greater Greensboro that he was making headway. He had nine months until the next request for proposals came out from the United Way, and in that short span of time, he had to come up with concrete results.

In the grant-making world, numbers matter a lot. As Peter Drucker put it in his 1999 book *The Drucker Foundation Self Assessment Tool: Participant Workbook*, "quantitative measures are essential for assessing whether resources are properly concentrated for results, whether progress is being made, whether lives and communities are changing for the better." Getting to the level of abstraction of Drucker's quote at which a new agency faces the challenge of building a lazy Susan is not easy. Odell had to convince numerous people, fast, to support his new operation and answer a survey. He had to learn names and faces, get to know different churches and their programs, and be prepared to shake hands and hug babies if or when he needed to pull a rabbit out of his hat. Such work on infrastructure is the hidden world beneath the visible evolution of program development in a human services system, and being able to know how, when, where, and how much to go up and down the ladder of abstractions is central. We had to get into that work quickly and prudently.

THE COMMUNITY ACTIVIST CALLS THE PROFESSOR TO LUNCH

Recently, Odell called me and guilt-tripped me into attending the annual luncheon of the Joseph M. Bryan Foundation, a major foundation in Greensboro that not only supports nonprofits but also uses civic organizational leadership to promote economic development. As a recipient of the foundation's support, Odell receives a yearly invitation and can bring a guest.

Thirteen years ago, the glove was on the other hand. Back then, I would invite Odell to meetings and workshops. There was one particularly memorable two-day organizational development retreat in rural northern Virginia. The retreat was for a black church that had bought an abandoned school to convert into a community center. The community was split over whether the center should be for adults, primarily for the elderly, or for the community's youths.

The Jessie Ball duPont Fund hired me to run the retreat and help the church community find common ground. The parallels were so numerous between what Odell was undertaking and what the church in Virginia was considering that he agreed to leave his young family (with their blessing, of course) for a weekend retreat in rural Virginia.

Odell could learn a framework for program development in a retreat much more quickly than in a piecemeal discussion here and there. While the community strategy was developing, he also was receiving a formal introduction to program development inside the organization and in a community setting. He saw early on how I went up and down the ladder of abstraction with community leadership and with the program officer of the duPont Fund, who was at the retreat as well. Later on, in our heated discussions about shaping a community story line, I would hearken back to that weekend.

The first person we met at the luncheon, and who we knew in common, was Reverend Mike Aiken, executive director of Greensboro Urban Ministry. Reverend Aiken, who was giving the luncheon invocation, was an early supporter of the Welfare Reform Liaison Project, especially in brokering Odell's first grant from the United Way and his second grant of $25,000 from First Presbyterian Church in Greensboro in 1998. Greensboro Urban Ministry receives support from around 350 of the community's congregations, and because congregants are also citizens, the ministry's work, especially in community development, spills into civic life as well.

Greensboro Urban Ministry is one of four agencies in Greensboro that is larger than life and a model for what I hoped the Welfare Reform Liaison Project to become. It was larger than life because Reverend Aiken's agency had institutional backing from 350 congregations, which translates into an ability to quickly mobilize five thousand people for the annual CROP Walk for the Hungry or turn out one thousand people for the annual interdenominational and multicultural community fund-raiser at Thanksgiving, proceeds of which go to pay for turkeys for low-income families.

As we were talking, Reverend Aiken had one ear for us and one eye for the rest of the room. As we parted, he said that he had to "be careful" with his prayer, so as not to offend anyone by making it "Christian centered"—the room was full of people who reflected the racial and religious diversity of Greensboro's public square. His invocation stayed at the highest level of abstraction and offended no one.

Odell smiled after Reverend Aiken walked away, and muttered, "That's easy," to me as we walked to our lunch table—"easy" meaning being careful about being inclusive with something as innocuous as a luncheon prayer. When I reminded Odell that his 1998 letter that accompanied the grant to the United Way ended "In His Service," he gave a good a laugh—"I don't do that anymore!"

Reverend Aiken knew Bessie the cow and the ladder of abstraction, too. Both pastors without pews—one white, one black—worked their way around the tables with handshakes and hugs. They were sealing the bonds they made over the years, a key factor in their organizational success. Greensboro Urban Ministry has become a symbol of the collective good of the religious community, kinds of religion aside. Moreover, the good people of the nonreligious community feel they can serve there without being excluded. It is a true community organization, and it operates on the principle of faith works, not faith talk. The Welfare Reform Liaison Project operates that way now, too.

Odell and Reverend Aiken got to where they are today by different routes, but with one commonality. In the early 1980s, Aiken took over a little storefront urban ministry and grew it into a multicampus, multiservice, multimillion-dollar agency and a key player in community social services and partnership development.

In 1988, Aiken and I surveyed the community's major white and black congregations to learn about what kind of partnerships they had with other agencies and what kinds of services they were providing on site. The Reagan-era budget cuts were pressuring congregations to serve their communities in much the same way that welfare reform of the 1990s and the recession of 2008–2010 did to force increasing numbers of hungry, homeless, and the unemployed to show up at church steps.

Around that time, the *Greensboro News and Record* ran a story reporting that the Greensboro Urban Ministry could not find volunteers to staff the night shelter for the homeless. The ministry was being forced to make people sleep in the streets. I was analyzing the data from our collective study at the time, and one question we had asked church leaders about was whether their congregations would be willing to help Urban Ministry at the night shelter. I called Reverend Aiken to tell him the names of the ten congregations that said they were willing to help. He called those church leaders and they agreed to help. In those early years, Odell had to build that kind of trust and community support—and get the data to help plan his agency, too.

GETTING QUALITATIVE DATA, SEALING CONNECTIONS, AND STRENGTHENING PARTNERSHIPS

In putting Drucker's idea about research into operation—that quantitative measures are important for community agencies because they give them factual foundation to move toward changing their community for the better—Odell also had to use his meetings to get qualitative data by learning in between the lines from each pastor and church he visited. One has only to go to a public event like the Welfare Reform Liaison Project's faith summit to see how the connections Odell made in the qualitative aspects of his survey research take form. Odell is always the master of ceremony at his events—the "magician of ceremony," actually. He stands at the podium larger than life as he digs down in his hat in the middle of his presentation and pulls out a reference to a discussion he had with this clergy person or that person ten years earlier. Then he connects those people to the Welfare Reform Liaison Project's successes, as if it were their doing alone. Maybe that's partly the case, but Odell makes it seem as if it all happened yesterday.

And that is why Odell wanted me to go to the luncheon, to remind his "bald-headed Jewish professor" that this work is not academic theory; it is handshakes and hugs in practice everyday—and he loves it, and he does it well. He is amazing. Odell constantly remortars his connections wherever he goes, even when he's at his desk. And he is never shy about reminding me to get out of the ivory tower and into the community, where the reality I teach about actually takes place. That day, he not only had dragged me from my desk; when I returned from the luncheon, I saw that my mentee-turned-teacher, Reverend Odell Cleveland, had already fired off four instructive e-mails to me. Each had something to do with a connection he had rekindled at lunch.

I noted earlier that the Bryan Foundation is very committed to the economic development of not just Greensboro but also the Piedmont Triad of North Carolina, a region with a population of 1.6 million people. As such, the foundation devoted its annual luncheon to promoting and informing the attendees about the importance of cooperative, regionally focused economic development. For the foundation's leaders, the region is a community of shared interests. But they also understand its role in building a strong civil society to form the backbone of economic development.

At the luncheon, Bobby Long, a speaker on economic development, talked about how we collectively needed to promote our region economically. That same speaker, Bobby Long, also headed up the Chrysler-Wyndham Greater Greensboro Golf Tournament. Part of the Professional Golfer's Association (PGA) tour, the tournament is run by a spin-off nonprofit organization spawned by the community's leading foundations, which use the proceeds from the tournament to showcase the community to the country and to corporate sponsors.

Three other presenters also reflected broadly on the foundation's community work. The first was the president of Guilford Technical Community College, the same president who gave the thumbs-up for his faculty to teach an on-site GED program for Odell's high-school-dropout program. He talked about the college's aviation technology program and its partnership with Honda Jet, a relatively new company in the region. He then introduced a student in the aviation program who had won a Honda Jet scholarship and a job while he earned a degree. Later, a high school math instructor in a low-income school and her student poignantly praised the foundation's efforts to supply the latest classroom technology for math instruction.

The student said that the Smart board, a computer-operated white board and spinoff of the blackboard of old, and other technological gadgetry helped transform him from a bored, uninvolved student into one who loves math. Odell's training program works with students who had not been turned on to education and had dropped out of high school. Before introducing his next presenter, the CEO of the foundation, a former mayor and highly regarded civic leader, cunningly chided the county commissioners and school board representatives at the luncheon for their fear of raising taxes for education—even if the taxes went for educational development in math, a major need in our region.

The executive director of Horsepower, to whom Odell had introduced me before lunch, runs an organization that works with disabled children. She spoke of her organization's work and was followed by a mom whose disabled child participated in the program. On any given day, one can find a job coach working at Odell's Job Training Distribution Center with a disabled student, preparing him or her for the workforce. The foundation's luncheon, in other words, was home court for Odell.

I FORGOT HOW NETWORKING AND ORGANIZING WORK

Odell's presence was a prompt to the foundation's leaders to invite him to an event tied to the Greensboro Golf Tournament. We reproduce the e-mail invitation here. Carole Bruce, the author of the e-mail, is an influential lawyer in Greensboro and a foundation leader. The invitation speaks for itself:

> **From:** Carole Bruce
> **Sent:** Thursday, February 11, 2010 2:06 PM
> **To:** Odell Cleveland
> **Subject:** The First Tee
> Dear Odell,
> I was pleased to see you at the Bryan Foundation meeting today and wanted to talk with you about The First Tee. I'm working with this group to help build a program in Greensboro. I hoped that you might be interested in learning more about this program and its impact on lives of young people. Please let me know if you can join us.

Much of the hand shaking and hugging came about as a result of building a community strategy that started with making connections. Initially those connections were private, but Odell keeps resealing them publicly. Eighty-two visits to clergy in Greensboro in 1998 and 1999 helped, as did our growing understanding of how the ladder of abstraction works in reality.

In 1998, while I brokered for the data expert to enter data and report the survey findings, Odell had to shoulder into the door, explaining a survey to the non-researchers who would answer it and developing a strategy that would be successful in bringing nonacademics to our new lazy Susan—we would become partners, giving to them and getting from them, so everyone benefits. This was a stormy period: welfare policy was confusing, and locally there was chaos in the employment-training field and job market. This chaotic and confused social services environment was challenging for a novice like Odell, but it also presented an enormous opportunity. As I told him many a time during those early days, in a crowd of the blind, a man with one eye is a visionary. And vision is something Odell certainly had in spades.

Odell had a new idea for addressing the chaos in the welfare system. First, though, he needed to understand the resources of the religious community, what congregations give to their members and the community through social programs— not just theology but also the religious community's role in the public square. And he needed to get that understanding himself, one church at a time. Success or failure of each church and church leader depended on the strength and sustainability of the partnerships that he or she aimed to develop.

Odell couldn't enter any church with a survey instrument and just collect data. He had a target on the horizon, and so to get the data—and build relationships— he went door-to-door like a census taker. His approach was more a sales call than an information-gathering session.

For an academic, data are often a means to build knowledge, increase publications, win grants, and earn respect among peers as a legitimate social scientist. I would eventually use the data to make academic presentations and write scholarly articles, but as an engaged scholar, the immediate gratification of university rewards was a distant second to working with Odell to invent the local future. The academy could wait—and it should.

Odell was sure we could pull this off. Winning the grant to undertake the project gave the experiential-oriented Odell enough evidence and money to believe that research would help the cause. He knew he could get in the door, and he started to understand how to talk to different people from different venues who were concerned with welfare and the role of religion in the public square.

Odell had made sales calls in his life before the ministry. But now he had to sell himself, sell his new agency, and sell his future programs to get three things from the survey respondents: trust, information, and his story line spread in a positive light throughout the religious community and into the public square in Greensboro. He, his agency, and his church were going to enter into the chaotic welfare services realm and eventually evolve into the broader workforce development sphere. Odell needed much more than data to succeed. He needed full-throttle support from everyone, everywhere. Quantitative data and quality relationships would need to go hand-in-hand.

A MAJOR INSIGHT: DATA CAN HELP AND MORE

One of the findings Odell was picking up as he went along with the survey assessment, a finding that jumped out at us during the analysis of the aggregate data, was that 90 percent of survey respondents, most of whom were spiritual leaders, subscribed to this statement: "Meeting the needs of the poor demands collaboration between public assistance (Department of Social Service), community support and church as partners in a common cause." We would see the seeds planted in 1999 sprout in the spring of 2010 in ways we could only dream of (see chapter 9).

I will never know what effect Odell had on shaping those results with his story line, his big smile, and his contagious passion, but I had evidence (which might not hold up under peer review for an academic journal) that there was a common philosophical foundation underpinning the building of partnerships in this community.

There was a common Greensboro cause, and church leaders would step out of their church doors to nurture the cause. Getting information was no problem for Odell—he talked his way into churches; he was passionate about his cause. He physically changes when he talks about his passion: helping. There is no doubt that he made connections easily and crafted the story line of collaboration, congregational responsibility, and the Welfare Reform Liaison Project that his ministerial brethren would spread.

On this journey, Odell picked up not only a board member but also a second funder, Mr. Mo Sellers of the First Presbyterian Church, along with a $25,000 contribution to the Welfare Reform Liaison Project from Mo Sellers's church. Following the typologies of the role of the congregation in public life, the First Presbyterian Church is what is known as a civic-oriented congregation. During the 1990s, the First Presbyterian Church did not have a great activist role in community affairs, but it did work quietly behind the scenes, contributing to the programmatic efforts of other agencies. Its members would be perceived as civic leaders who were board members of agencies, and so, if one were not familiar with the congregation, it would appear that the church led in a civic way indistinguishable from public service.

In the 1980s, before the current junior U.S. senator from North Carolina Kay Hagan was in politics, she was an active civic leader; she even invited me to speak to her Sunday school class in 1989, right after my survey results from the study with the Greensboro Urban Ministry became public. The morning after that class, I received a call from the president of the United Way to schedule a meeting. It turned out that Kay Hagan's husband, Chip, was the president of the board of directors of the United Way of Greater Greensboro, and he had been at my presentation.

I learned a great number of lessons that day about community power; about how the mainline, civic-oriented white congregations educate themselves on Sundays, and how that line between congregants and genuinely community-minded leaders blurs on Monday. The more research I did, the more I understood that people from all types of religious groups, not just powerful white congregations, but black congregations and non-Christian religions as well, interchange their individual religious and secular community roles on Sundays and Mondays to help organizations in the public square partner with their congregations.

I have been criticized in academic circles, even by my friends, that this claim of mine is bigger than warranted. They said I was talking about only one community in the Bible Belt. However, national research undertaken by Mark Chaves of Duke University, as well as the Delaware study I noted previously, have put such criticisms to rest. Chaves's work showed that, in any given community, about half of congregations partner with community-service-providing organizations. Our work in Delaware was more local and thus more specific. We found that more than half of congregations—227 of 440—provided United Way and public agencies with volunteers, goods, money, and/or use of their facilities. These partnerships are organic. Parties do not exchange a lot of money, and the process can become stronger if done mindfully.

The one thing I learned about the local use of research is that it often looks nothing like it does in journals, and what happens as a result of research done in the community for the community deserves a bit more elaboration. Mr. Mo Sellers, a retired outreach and influential super volunteer of the First Presbyterian Church, was so impressed by what Odell was saying at a community meeting that he developed a relationship with Odell that eventually led to his brokering of the Welfare Reform Liaison Project's second grant of $25,000 from the First Presbyterian Church. Mr. Sellers also became a member of the founding board of directors.

During the latter part of the 1990s and into the first decade of the new millennium, the First Presbyterian Church became more action minded in the community, especially in service development, advocacy, and civic involvement. Kay Hagan became a state senator and championed programs for children across the state, which benefited our community greatly. The congregation developed a drop-in center in the neighboring community for HIV-positive people, and it later gave the operation over to the United Way agency that serves this group and group members' families. Today the church also runs a nightly food program at its facilities for anyone who is hungry, because its members could not sit idle during the recession of 2008–2010 as people knocked on its doors for help. It also opened a night shelter in the winter months for the homeless.

GOOD KARMA

There is another bit of good karma in this story worth recounting.

Dick Bruce, the husband of Carole Bruce—the lawyer who e-mailed Odell the invite to the First Tee event—began a second career in employment assistance at the First Presbyterian Church, where he established a new nonprofit that helps members of the congregation and others find work and develop new careers—the recession has hit the First Presbyterian Church, too.

By now the reader should have a pretty good grasp of how the interlocking networks operate locally. The little guys seek help from the big guys, who, if impressed by the little guys, help financially and with other resources. They get connected, and the connections, if nurtured properly, grow stronger.

Dick Bruce turned to Odell for help in workforce program development, and Odell obliged, much like Mo Sellers responded to Odell in 1998. And although we won't try to assume or guess blindly, we're both comfortable saying that had Odell not sold Sellers on his mission thirteen years earlier, the Welfare Reform Liaison Project would not have been able to bless the First Presbyterian Church's earlier generosity with $10,000 worth of consultations and $15,000 in seed money.

In the beginning, the United Way of Greater Greensboro and the First Presbyterian Church helped get the fledgling Welfare Reform Liaison Project off the ground. Today, Odell is a board member of United Way and sits on its finance committee, and his agency, which once received money from the First Presbyterian Church, is now compensating their generosity in kind.

CHAPTER 5

Getting Fred Newman on the Bus

*In this chapter, we once again go out of chronological order because
in the following chapters we start to deal with the very sensitive financial and racial
issues in Greensboro. Although Fred Newman changed the racial dynamics of the
Welfare Reform Liaison Program's leadership team, we did not want to distract
from the racial and community dynamics of our story by returning to a key piece of
internal organizational development after we dealt with race. This chapter is
about how important it was for Odell to get a key player on his team and less
directly about finances and race, although we will come back to Fred's
importance to the project after this chapter.*

GROWTH MEANS A NEED FOR MORE DISCIPLINED LEADERSHIP

Complex social service organizations need different leadership styles in different parts of the organization at different stages of their development. They also need leaders who can be creative risk takers one moment and narrowly focused bookkeepers the next—and who can sometimes switch between the two from one minute to the next.

Odell Cleveland was not yet that kind of leader when the Welfare Reform Liaison Project started out in 1998 with the $25,000 grant from the United Way's Bryan Community Enrichment and Venture Grant Program, but in the years since, he has adapted to changing circumstances over and over and over again. A right-brained visionary by nature, Odell learned what he could and could not do as a leader, and he adjusted the internal workings of his organization accordingly.

He took the discipline he had learned early on in life—the discipline that helped him lead his college basketball team to a national championship and then become a highly successful salesman—and incorporated it into his ministerial and nonprofit leadership practices. That discipline got the Welfare Reform Liaison Project off the ground and led Odell to recognize that he needed an organizational overseer—a master of the nuts and bolts—to avoid internal financial chaos, which, in Greensboro at least, would inevitably have been portrayed as yet another black church wasting the community's resources.

There was no doubt that God was driving Odell, but to paraphrase management expert Jim Collins, he still needed to get the right people on his fast-moving bus—specifically, Fred Newman, Greensboro's most respected community steward, given his more than thirty years in the United Way system and eighteen-plus years as vice president of community impact at the United Way of Greater Greensboro.

We talk more about Fred and how he got on Odell's bus later. But first, a word or two about Odell's discipline: Odell is the kind of guy who always flies on US Airways instead of Southwest Airlines, knowing full well that he will have to pay extra for the cost of his ticket and checked luggage. He is willing to pay more so that he can reserve his seat. He wants to choose ahead of time which seat he will sit in, and Southwest doesn't offer him the assurances that his discipline demands.

Like most busy travelers, Odell would love to sleep, do office work, or chat while on flights. But instead, he makes it a point to read US Airways' in-flight magazine—"The Magazine That Connects You," as it's billed. His reasoning for that habit is that he often finds innovative ideas in the magazine, which he then digests and translates into action. On a business trip ten years ago, he found these guiding words in the magazine: "In business, you don't get what you deserve, you get what you negotiate." He cut out the caption and to this day keeps it on his desk as a reminder that he has to work hard to win, just like he did in his basketball days when he was an undersized center.

It is that discipline that has driven Odell to success in all his endeavors, be they athletic, business, or social service. One is not entitled to victory just by suiting up for the game. One must play the game, and with a purpose. Discipline by itself did not deliver Odell Cleveland to where he is today, but it did position him to make the right decisions along the way.

Discipline, as the vignette here by Jim Collins illustrates, is what transformed the Welfare Reform Liaison Project from dreams and prayers into a great workforce development corporation, all in the span of just a few years.

> We must reject the idea—well-intentioned, but dead wrong—that the primary path to greatness in the social sectors is to become "more like a business." Most businesses—like most of anything else in life—fall somewhere between mediocre and good. Few are great. When you compare great companies with good ones, many widely practiced business norms turn out to correlate with mediocrity, not greatness. So, then, why would we want to import the practices of mediocrity into the social sectors?
>
> I shared this perspective with a gathering of business CEOs, and offended nearly everyone in the room. A hand shot up from David Weekley, one of the more thoughtful CEOs—a man who built a very successful company

and who now spends nearly half his time working with the social sectors. "Do you have evidence to support your point?" he demanded. "In my work with nonprofits, I find that they're in desperate need of greater discipline—disciplined planning, disciplined people, disciplined governance, disciplined allocation of resources."

"What makes you think that's a business concept?" I replied. "Most businesses also have a desperate need for greater discipline. Mediocre companies rarely display the relentless culture of discipline—disciplined people who engage in disciplined thought and who take disciplined action—that we find in truly great companies. A culture of discipline is not a principle of business; it is a principle of greatness."

Later, at dinner, we continued our debate, and I asked Weekley: "If you had taken a different path in life and become, say, a church leader, a university president, a nonprofit leader, a hospital CEO, or a school superintendent, would you have been any less disciplined in your approach? Would you have been less likely to practice enlightened leadership, or put less energy into getting the right people on the bus, or been less demanding of results?" Weekley considered the question for a long moment. "No, I suspect not."

—Jim Collins, *Good to Great and the Social Sectors*

At first glance, the Welfare Reform Liaison Project might appear to outsiders to be a case study in what organizational literature has termed *founders' syndrome*. Founders' syndrome, according to Carter McNamara's *Field Guide to Developing and Operating Your Nonprofit Board of Directors*, "occurs when, rather than working toward its overall mission, the organization operates primarily according to the personality of a prominent person in the organization." Odell himself would agree with parts of that characterization. But things at the Welfare Reform Liaison Project are more complex than the archetype suggests, in large part because of Odell's relentless discipline.

As Odell became more successful in the community, earning increasing legitimacy and correspondingly more funds to develop programs, my energy revolved mainly around constructing a disciplined community strategy to develop a stakeholder base, to provide technical assistance in securing funds, and (to a far lesser degree) to offer help with daily internal organizational management needs.

I suggested a person Odell might hire as the lead case manager and began to place student interns at the agency to help them learn about the "new style of helping"—on-site classroom and simulated work experiences in the Job Training Distribution Center—and assist the staff in administrative and organizational matters, but I did not take part in the hiring process. Nor did I participate in setting criteria for client selection, goal setting, staff evaluations, or curriculum development for the training classes.

I did conduct a board orientation and helped define the committee structure, but I did not work with the board as completely as I had with other organizations, for which I helped develop one-year and five-year plans, assigned people to appropriate committees, and set up working task groups. In those instances of other organizations, such involvement on my part was called for, but for various reasons, with the Welfare Reform Liaison Project, it was best for me to play a background role.

As the agency grew, Odell, like countless other organizational founders, faced the increasingly difficult task of surrounding himself with personnel who could help drive the operation forward. Getting the right people on the team is a challenge under any circumstances. But when the bus is already moving and trying to pick up speed, as was the case with the Welfare Reform Liaison Project, the challenge is far more dynamic—what Jim Collins refers to in *Good to Great and the Social Sectors* as "getting the right people on the bus within social sector constraints." In Odell's case, the social sector constraints came hard and fast from the beginning, and the fact that they were both internal and external made them doubly difficult.

The Welfare Reform Liaison Project's board of directors evolved from Mount Zion Baptist Church, Greensboro's largest African-American congregation. Its leaders knew that I, a white Jewish professor, was advising Odell, but there was no doubt that the Welfare Reform Liaison Project was an organization run by African Americans for African Americans.

When Odell came on the scene, the church was emerging from being centered on the neighborhood and emergency assistance and was going forth into the broader community. Odell's entrance was further complicated by the fact that another nonprofit in the area, also led by an African-American minister and one that had received large sums of money from the city toward low-income housing, was being investigated for fraudulent practices.

On the one hand, the Welfare Reform Liaison Project's faith-centeredness helped get it off the ground, because it linked the program with a congregation viewed as trouble free in the community's eyes. Yet the same faith-centeredness—which, it must be noted, was always complemented by hardworking, highly dedicated, casework-oriented staff—gave the early Welfare Reform Liaison Project the look and feel of an African-American community ministry. The commitment of its staff—who showed a sense that this was more than just a job—was of the kind more often associated with religious efforts than with secular nonprofits.

Both Odell and his new staff had a religious spirit that was steeped in helping the community's most unfortunate. As recently as 2001, Odell still signed his written correspondences "In His Service." But everyone's common commitment to Jesus would eventually come to a head—not over ends, as might be expected, but over means.

Personalities may have been a factor in the organizational clash, but external demands for accountability made client outcomes even more of a driving force than they might otherwise have been. Those demands for accountability stemmed in large part from a very real social sector constraint: communal suspicion bred by the afore-mentioned fraud investigation into a fellow African-American-led nonprofit in Greensboro.

The demand for a disciplined operation, however, was hardly an external impo-sition. From the beginning, Odell aimed for a case management system based on con-tractual relationships rather than the entitlement relationships so often found in similar organizations. His view has always been that the Welfare Reform Liaison Project should provide a hand up and not a hand out.

I remember one instance when I, the good liberal willing to toss thirteen feet of rope to someone twenty feet off shore, was struck dumb by Odell's insistence on holding everyone and all to the same standard. In one of his personal development classes, a student showed up one minute late, not a second more. He told her to leave the class and said she was welcome to join the next sixteen-week session if she were willing to play by his rules.

Far from being heartless, his rationale was clear and concise. His program was voluntary, and he was training people to abide by the strictest rules of corporate America, which in the South means this: "If you are black and you screw up, you're out. Period."

He also had his funders to report to. He had to inform them that X number of people were making Y amount of progress, and so he insisted on a linear progress grid for each student. It was Odell who was brokering people into jobs, and his rep-utation was on the line. The aggregate success of the Welfare Reform Liaison Project would give funders the incentive to help the program help even more participants.

All the hand shaking and back slapping, Odell was quickly learning, meant nothing without measurable results. The community wanted discipline when it came to spending philanthropic and public dollars, especially when those were being spent on an upstart organization that was emerging from a black church in Greensboro.

But while Odell was being logical, linear, and left-brained in making demands of his casework staff, the staff itself operated on a far different model, one that assumed that when people saw the light and heard the call, they would instantly begin the journey to self-sufficiency.

Time and accountability—what Odell demanded from himself and what the com-munity demanded from the Welfare Reform Liaison Project—were lower-order con-cepts for much of his staff. Steeped in the church culture from which the Welfare Reform Liaison Project had emerged, staff processed their caseloads with the belief that anyone and everyone could eventually be helped, regardless of where they were on the road to self-sufficiency.

The work culture was a constraint both internal and external, which made it particularly challenging in the early years. Internally, the organization was struggling between being a program of the church and one from the church. An entire day, sometimes two, might be spent taking someone to and from work at the expense of other lesser needs of clients. The same balancing act was also playing out externally. To gain legitimacy in the community, the Welfare Reform Liaison Project initially had to project itself as cut from the same cloth as the well-regarded Mount Zion Baptist Church. But to acquire a more lasting sense of communal legitimacy, Odell had to prove to his benefactors that the Welfare Reform Liaison Project was a cost-effective, results-oriented, welfare-to-work program—a far different beast than the church's traditional help-all-those-in-need efforts.

The challenge before Odell was a daunting one: he had to successfully integrate faith-based social services into a web of essential institutional partnerships and provide help for those in need in ways that could empirically demonstrate to funders and the broader community that the Welfare Reform Liaison Project met their definitions of success.

An anecdote I heard and recorded well after the Welfare Reform Liaison Project had found its feet captures the fundamental difference between the clashing intervention strategies Odell was facing. Dr. Richard "Skip" Moore, director of the Weaver Foundation in Greensboro, told the story during a speech at the dedication of the Welfare Reform Liaison Project's current home, a new seventy-two-thousand-square-foot social service, education, training and distribution center:

> I said to Odell, "The Weaver Foundation is going to give you $100,000 to get this training center started."
> Odell gasped and said, "It's a gift from God!"
> "Yeah," I reminded him, "but it is through the Weaver Foundation—and you better remember that!"

In those early years, my role was best kept in the background, for several reasons. It simply wasn't kosher for a guy like me—a white Jewish professor from the local white university—to be visibly involved with the governance structure or program operation of an African-American organization in Greensboro. The most that could be tolerated was a peek-a-boo presence, like leading a board retreat or attending a growth and development class once a week. Odell and I were comfortable with the arrangement—and we talked almost every day.

Simply put, internally, the Welfare Reform Liaison Project did not need my white face to be part of its identity and self-description. I had been in Greensboro since 1980 and had already had some experience with the smoldering racial tensions, which were never far below the surface.

Odell handled any questions about my presence. Not that he didn't have his own, of course. "Why would God put this bald-headed Jewish professor in my life?" he asked himself. He wasn't scheming to shape the story line; he really believed it and still does.

My role was to make sure Odell heard me while as few people as possible saw me. Odell would handle the reality of a non-Christian white guy at his side, and he would do so on his own Christian terms.

I was not the only white Jewish guy, however, to have an impact on the Welfare Reform Liaison Project. It would be a few years before he got on the bus, but eventually Odell picked up one of his most important passengers of all, Fred Newman.

THE UNITED WAY'S NUMBER-ONE COMMUNITY MAN

When the Welfare Reform Liaison Project was just starting out, Fred Newman was already a household name in Greensboro's social service community. He was the vice president of community impact at Greensboro's United Way, and when it came to the grant-making process there, he was the real force behind the scenes. He was the one who ensured that every organizational grantee filed its evaluation reports and financial statements on time, and he often kept those organizations out of ruts that would have hindered their development. He added his disciplined organizational and community leadership experience to the very good management team that was in place at Welfare Reform Liaison Project. His hiring was a decision that Bishop Brooks, senior pastor of Mount Zion Baptist Church and cofounder of Welfare Reform Liaison Project, blessed beforehand! The Welfare Reform Liaison Project, birthed out of the spiritual womb of Mount Zion Baptist Church, had hired Fred, a prominent member of Greensboro's Jewish community, for a leadership position at the project that was now on its way to being of the community.

I first got to know Fred in the 1980s and knew how he operated. In 1990, I succeeded in helping what is now a mainstay Greensboro agency plan and in gaining membership in the United Way. Fred and I had worked with Volunteers in Service to America (Vista) during the same era. Our training as community organizers was grounded in management by objectives and in how the implementation of objectives worked inside an organization with an eye on community impact.

The organization that I helped was the one that had taken over the administration of the First Presbyterian Church's drop-in center for people with HIV and AIDS. Fred knew all about such complicated community partnerships and the role of staff development in them. Over the years, he has shaped many such arrangements and guided organizations through rough transition times.

Fred Newman became Greensboro's symbol for nonprofit organizational accountability, both in the community and inside the United Way system. He ensured that the United Way delivered on its responsibilities and lived up to its mission, and he oversaw how grantee agencies were using United Way's money. As the vice president of community impact, Fred was always trying to keep everyone going in the same direction, be it through communication or through designing systems to accomplish agency and United Way goals harmoniously.

In Fred's world, an organization could do anything, but it could not do everything. Right-brainers, like Odell when he received his first grant, think they can do anything and everything, and initially Odell was not attuned to a Fred Newman–type of logic and discipline.

Formal study before designing a program or systematic monitoring of overall progress were both new territory for Odell. But he knew that data mattered. And he knew that his case-management style, based on self-help and accountability, was the way to go. That put him at odds with the more right-brained, faith-centered case-workers who staffed the Welfare Reform Liaison Project. The internal system there was being pulled in different directions.

For a while, Odell was able to balance things. He was a right-brained visionary externally and a left-brained manager internally. I was his part-time Fred Newman, helping out when left and right brain couldn't come to an agreement.

But as the program grew, the tension became more untenable. The Welfare Reform Liaison Project was becoming larger than life in the community, but from within, it was slowly being pulled apart because of growing demand for admission into the program from potential students and because funders were asking the project to serve more students for the funds it was giving them.

As the organization's budget increased, the juggling act Odell was performing— growing a program with his left brain and being the ambassador of a new brand with his right—increasingly tilted in favor of program development. But program development simply could not be accomplished in a Fred Newman–like way without someone inside the organization making it happen hourly. In just one year, the budget from all funding sources had more than doubled, from $196,000 to $450,000. Money was pouring in, as were growing demands for more bang for the buck.

Had Odell just been selling contracts in the trucking business, the Fred Newmans of the firm, not Odell himself, would have handled the logistics of shipping, invoicing, paying bills, and generating quarterly and annual reports. But the Welfare Reform Liaison Project, of course, was not the trucking business, although today one might wonder as much having witnessed several eighteen-wheelers moving in and out of the Distribution Center on any given day.

As part of another research project, I had been collecting data from other sources, including community support teams from churches across North Carolina, and I saw the handwriting on Odell's wall. The bureaucracy that the Welfare Reform

Liaison Project faced was too complex for a small staff with already-increasing caseloads to handle competently.

In my research inside the Welfare Reform Liaison Project, I found that the number of major bureaucratic hurdles the staff had to lower before women could get a full-time job averaged three per person. The women had child-care problems, including caring for children with medical problems or a reading level sometimes no higher than first or second grade. They couldn't meet the rent or had no means of transportation to work if a job did become available to them.

The caseworkers, in the statewide study I conducted during that period, who had volunteer support teams to help those in need with such concerns were burning out—and fast. But not as fast as the volunteer support teams they enlisted from churches. The American social service referral system has never been, and will never be, a one-stop service shop like the British system. So, a large policy change like the 1996 welfare reform, whose new mandate—"no work no eat"—hardly addressed the complex problems women faced, had unintended and harmful consequences for everyone. It would take new models of partnerships among welfare agencies, community support organizations, the recipients of service, and innovators like Odell to reconfigure services to gain some balance to address the new changes with solemnity.

The challenges Odell faced after the Welfare Reform Liaison Project received its first grant of $25,000 were similar to those most new nonprofit leaders face. He had to do the work promised in the grant, he had to raise more funds to get the program up and running, and he had to hire staff and recruit clients. And with the Clinton administration flipping the welfare-to-work bureaucracy on its head, Odell had to accomplish all those things while operating in a chaotic and rapidly changing environment.

At least money was not the problem that it is at many fledging nonprofits. Odell's personality, combined with communitywide confusion about what to do with mothers who were being pushed off welfare and into the workforce unprepared, actually helped funds flow into the Welfare Reform Liaison Project. A few months after that first grant was awarded in 1998, Odell received $25,000 from Mo Sellers, another $25,000 and a donated car from the Bryan Family Fund, and a state contract for $212,000 to move people rapidly off the welfare rolls and into the workforce.

It was an exciting time at the Annex, a well-groomed, one-story brick house right across the street from Mount Zion Baptist Church. There was more than enough room to have dedicated space for classrooms, an area for interviewing prospective participants, and staff offices. The church covered Odell's salary, and the Annex was space "donated" by the church.

Contacts Odell had made in the business world, as well as church members or their contacts, were willing to partner in supervised job placement. There was a

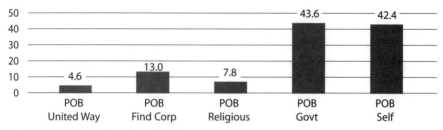

Note: *POB stands for percentage of agency budget*

FIGURE 4. *United Way of Delaware Budget Breakdown*

sixteen-week personal growth class, a pre-job-training class that Odell taught, and a computer skills training class through Guilford Technical Community College. Within a year, there would be a GED program, also in partnership with Guilford Tech; job-placement services; and the stretched case-management services.

The Welfare Reform Liaison Project's simulated distribution job-training program, the centerpiece of its efforts today, was being run out of a two-car garage. With the megachurch visible in the background, it is not overstatement to say that the Annex was filled with the spirit of the Lord. The bookkeeper was a church employee, and Odell was a minister of the church. One of the three caseworkers was a Mount Zion member who would later become a minister; the second was active in her own church. The third was a well-respected social worker who for more than a decade had led Greensboro Urban Ministry's Project Independence, a program that matched welfare recipients with congregational support teams. A committed and experienced casework staff was in place. Things looked golden.

But what Odell didn't understand at the time is that in a nonprofit's launch phase, the gold standard in successful program development is stable, long-term funding. Research on nonprofit agency stability has shown that successful programs have at least five or six funding sources, and my own recent research couldn't have verified earlier studies more clearly.

Figure 4 shows a budget breakdown from twenty-five United Way of Delaware partner agencies—newer agencies like the Welfare Reform Liaison Project. The five budget categories from left to right show the multiple streams of funding, which include United Way funding; corporate and foundation grants; funds from the religious community; state, federal, and local government support; and self-support, which includes membership drives, different fund-raisers, donations, and entrepreneurial efforts. The biggest funding streams were government and self-help efforts. My advice over and over to Odell was to avoid putting all his eggs in one funding basket.

BUSINESS BRAIN, NONPROFIT SOUL

Odell was new to human services, new to United Way grant making, new to government grant and contract making, new to the foundation world, new to the religious funding world, and new to internal program development. He was so business oriented, in fact, that he had his students read Steven Covey's business bible, *The 7 Habits of Highly Effective People*. In corporate America, he reasoned, even those working in the basement should learn the traits that got those on the top floor to where they are. That was far different from any welfare-to-work approach that the Department of Social Services' new job developers were using.

Odell went so far as to become a certified Covey Business Trainer, a title that cost him $5,000 in training. Reverend Odell Cleveland was all business at a time when welfare changes needed that kind of mentality. My job, and later Fred Newman's job, was to get Odell to understand how the nonprofit business world operated and to satisfy his religious mission of winning for the poor.

Eventually, Odell's dual faith in business and God and his disciplined approach to human service clashed with the faith-centered case management model his staff used. But he was building momentum by building his own hand-up brand, and soon enough the awards and tributes started coming in, including a place in Harvard Divinity School's Summer Leadership Institute.

Odell was a fresh face in the community, with fresh ideas about solving old problems. His church, meanwhile, was shifting programmatically from emergency assistance to community-building efforts. The left-brain-oriented human services community would eventually catch up to Odell's out-of-the-box ways, and he, in turn, would learn their ways, with a little help from me every once in a while.

Odell was no amateur, though, when it came to understanding how to jostle with corporate people, a mind-set that was completely foreign to Greensboro's social services community. He was catching on to the fact that permanent, stable funding was a key to his agency's overall success. He needed to catch on quickly, because the funding realities of a new nonprofit soon would hit him. What follows is an example of hardball local politics and of the difference between theoretical discussions of welfare policy and how things actually play out on the ground.

In 1999, the Welfare Reform Liaison Project received a $212,000 state contract, mentioned earlier, to move people off welfare and into the workforce. Three months into the contract, however, the funds still had not been dispersed, and Odell needed to meet payroll. Around the same time, Guilford County's Department of Social Services (Greensboro is the county seat) wanted to contract out some of its training to the Welfare Reform Liaison Project. On July 1, the department, which had to ensure minimum job training for up to twelve weeks, offered the cash-strapped

Welfare Reform Liaison Project $10,000 to provide training and case management services for seventy-five women

At first the $10,000 looked inviting. But after looking carefully at items A through H and itemizing the true cost of the services the organization would agree to provide, we realized that Odell would need to outlay as much as $75,000 in staff time. The contract developers at the Department of Social Services must have known that it would cost them upward of $100,000 to provide the same services. This is how cost shifting operates and how the competition for scarce funds in a politically charged local policy environment actually plays out.

We concluded that the Welfare Reform Liaison Project did not have the capacity to deliver the services at the level the contract specified, and that if the organization accepted the offer, it would be under far more financial and programmatic pressure than it had been before the contract. We walked through a very plausible scenario, given the dynamics of our community at the time, that covered what would happen if we were to accept the contract.

We took a careful look at item J in the proposed contract: "To retain all books, records and other documents relevant to this Contract for period of (4) years after payments or until all audits continued beyond this period are completed." Say the Welfare Reform Liaison Project accepted the $10,000 and soon realized it needed more funds to deliver on the agreement. The three-person staff, which was deeply involved with each "voluntary client" who came into the program, would have to start spending more time trying to get money and would have less time to work with the substantially greater number of participants.

What was once a successful but limited operation would falter rapidly, and all of Greensboro would be watching. Some very conservative county commissioners surely would have wanted to make sure people were working and would have eventually demanded to see an audit. In their eyes, the story would have been that yet another African-American faith-based initiative may well have wasted $10,000 of public monies. We understood this possibility all too well, and the Welfare Reform Liaison Project worked with its lawyer to craft a realistic counterproposal. It would take nearly eleven more years before this partnership with the Department of Social Services came into being.

Fortunately—by the grace of God, in Odell's view—Dr. Alvin and Mrs. Tracey Powell showed up at the agency unannounced with a smile and a money order in the amount of $5,000. The Powells were Mount Zion church members and knew Odell and his wife from back when Odell was the parent-teacher association's president at Bennett College's Children House day care, where both the Powells' and the Clevelands' children went. Along with some other funds, the $10,000 that would have come from the Department of Social Services was almost covered.

The political pressure the Department of Social Services faced to get people to work at the lowest cost possible, combined with the inexperience of a new player in the public sphere, was a formula for failure. Worse yet, it could have been a way for latent racism to subtly rear its ugly head. It was not such a stretch to imagine that the same people who pushed for local churches in our community to take over welfare programs would be the first to say that this African-American faith-based organization should never have been entrusted with taxpayers' dollars to begin with. Odell had to juggle some very hot potatoes while walking on thin black ice.

There was quite a bit of political posturing around the Clinton-era welfare reform and around George W. Bush's faith-based initiatives several years later, but much of that was shadowboxing between the two sides of the church-state debate. There was scant regard for the practical ramifications of sending congregations and new organizations like the Welfare Reform Liaison Project into the scramble for decreasing funds.

Competition for scarce resources at the community level produces territoriality like that found in medieval fiefdoms and academic departments. And as this example demonstrates, the competition for scarce funds undermines the impetus for thoughtful planning and coordination, which is absolutely essential for handling the effects brought on by policy changes pushed out to the local level. The congregations and faith-based organizations that policy makers wanted so desperately to be elixirs for the nation's complex social ills simply did not have the skills or capacity to handle the problems they were being forced to address.

The Welfare Reform Liaison Project would eventually be able to do what policy makers had been asking for in the late 1990s, but only after internal changes had transformed the agency. First, in 2002, the Welfare Reform Liaison Project's budget increased threefold. Shortly thereafter, Fred Newman joined Odell's staff.

CHAPTER 6

What Does Quality of Performance Have to Do with the Color of Water?

Agencies must be aware that they can shape their destiny but that destiny can shape them. Odell and I, while we fought over strategies and tactics, always wanted to make sure that the standard by which the Welfare Reform Liaison Project was judged had nothing to do with race and everything to do with performance.

TWEETS

Back in the 1970s, when my wife and I were Vista volunteers, we lived in Blackfoot, Montana, population 127. There was one phone in the community, and the nearest town, Browning, was twelve miles away. Still, everyone there seemed to know everyone else's business. It was the reality of small-town rural life, and the actual truth was often subservient to the prevailing story line. Our friend Harold Butterfly called this information system the moccasin telegraph. The Greensboro social services world that the Welfare Reform Liaison Project entered in 1998 was its own little Blackfoot, as Odell was quickly finding out.

The accountability model that funders of all stripes were seeking demanded a lower unit cost—that means that the Welfare Reform Liaison Project had to serve more people, period. And it had to do so while developing a reputation as an organization that cared for its patrons and provided service differently in spirit and practice than did public welfare service providers.

It was within these types of constraints that Odell continually had to sell his agency to the community. Greensboro may have been a city of 250,000, in a county of 500,000, but the local social service community was a small town of interlocking agencies, organizations, and people doing the daily business of helping others in need. As new members of that community in 1998, we wanted to be accepted by it and simultaneously to shape it. That was no easy task.

As we demonstrated in the introduction to this book, the Welfare Reform Liaison Project has numerous partnerships. The volunteers come from religious congregations, universities and colleges, the courts, businesses, and private individuals—all of whom want to help. Funds stream in from an array of philanthropic, government, and individual tributaries. Institutions and organizations purchase memberships to the retail outlet at the Job Training Distribution Center. So even though many people shop there, they do so under the auspices of their sponsoring organizations. For example, foster parents might shop in the retail center and educators might come to the teacher warehouse for classroom supplies. So although thousands may help, and thousands more are served directly and indirectly, the Welfare Reform Liaison Program brokers only several hundred institutional connections with "real" contracts, which it seals regularly with handshakes and hugs. Greensboro's social service sector, at the community level, is a small town—and today Odell could be its mayor.

Trying to manage the story line that pervades the human services sector is essential, and it doesn't always read the way one would want. In the human services sector, there is not just the daily chatter that makes a story line; there are also the newsletters and Web sites that many congregations, nonprofit organizations, and public agencies put out. Today's organization might have a hard-copy newsletter, an electronic newsletter, a Facebook page, a Twitter account, or any number of other social-networking media outlets. Tweets are everywhere.

The exponential growth of information sources has made shaping the story line of the Welfare Reform Liaison Project and its role in the community a truly daunting task. Even when the story being told is full of praise, as the United Way's quarterly newsletter *Your Way* attests, less than completely accurate wording can have an outsized impact on communal perception (figure 5).

The United Way of Greater Greensboro sent *Your Way* out to leaders of the more than one thousand organizations in the business community and other sectors that contribute to the agency. From our point of view, the story was almost perfect. With carefully focused lenses, one can see its pluses. The newsletter talks about the Welfare Reform Liaison Project in the context of partnerships; its subtext was the policy concern of the day, "moving women on welfare into self-sufficiency." It didn't have to use the phrase "black women" in the text, as the picture replaced a thousand words by showing them handling boxes, not driving Cadillacs, as the stereotype went back then. And the quote at the end of the article, from a participant in the program, captured perfectly the spirit of the Welfare Reform Liaison Project: "They care about you and that makes me feel good. I'm gonna make it!"

Meanwhile, the picture of two black men unloading a truck full of donated goods suggested that the program was broader than a women's program—and it was indeed broader. A small percentage of single fathers were on welfare too, and the voluntary program attracted a few men from its inception.

To top it all off, the article presented Odell's vision about the Job Training Distribution Center as a reality, even though it would be years before it reached its

United Way
of Greater Greensboro

January-March, 1999

United Way forms Partnership to Promote Self-Sufficiency

The partnership means that the items can be shipped to Greensboro at a reduced rate and then inventoried, warehoused and distributed to area nonprofits through the Welfare Reform Liaison Project.

United Way of Greater Greensboro has formed a partnership with the Welfare Reform Liaison Project to bring needed resources to the community while at the same time teaching job skills that will enable families to become self-sufficient.

The partnership is a win-win situation for United Way and WLRP, which is a program sponsored by Mt. Zion Baptist Church. By joining together, men and women are getting the job training they need in order to support themselves and their families while at the same time individuals who could not afford to purchase necessary products are receiving them through area agencies.

Through United Way of America's Gifts In Kind program, your local United Way is able to access new products such as clothing, educational tools, software, and personal care items that can be distributed by area agencies. By joining forces with the WRLP, United Way has access to warehouse facilities as well as personnel with transportation and distribution experience.

Individuals enrolled in the twelve-week program learn the skills necessary to

work in a warehouse and receive assistance in overcoming barriers such as transportation and childcare that have kept them from succeeding at previous jobs. They also receive assistance in securing employment and case management services for eighteen months once they have completed the program to ensure that graduates become self-sufficient.

One program participant said she was grateful for the opportunity to get job skills training. "They (the Welfare Reform Liaison staff) push you. You're gonna learn if you want to graduate from this program. They care about you and that makes me feel good. I'm gonna make it!" ∎

FIGURE 5: *United Way Newsletter Article on the Welfare Reform Liaison Project*

true potential. Although the program was in its infancy and had just moved to a sixteen-thousand-square-foot warehouse, the article emphasized that the United Way of Greater Greensboro supported the Welfare Reform Liaison Project as a partner that had "transportation and distribution expertise," going so far as to call the partnership a win-win situation. (In the next chapter, we illustrate what win-win means in a community setting. The phrase "transportation and distribution expertise," it ought to be noted, is key to understanding the Welfare Reform Liaison Project's success, and we will come back to it later in this chapter.) But even in such a lauda-tory article, there was a small phrase that, left unattended, could very well have derailed the Welfare Reform Liaison Project's hard-earned communal story line.

Although a year earlier Odell had to impress on the grant committee that first funded the Welfare Reform Liaison Project that the agency was its own 501(c)3, the 501(c)3 line didn't stick the way I had hoped. We devote more to the issue of race, religion, and the black church here and in chapters 8 and 9. The United Way article, from our point of view, set out the Welfare Reform Liaison Project as a program of the church, not a new organization independent of the church. The article clearly noted, "The partnership is a win-win situation for the United Way and the Welfare Reform Liaison Project, which is a program sponsored by Mount Zion Baptist Church."

In another context, words might not be such a big deal, but even in the Bible Belt South, especially in Greensboro's public human services square, some major foundations do not fund churches.

WHOSE TWEET IS MOST IMPORTANT?

The Weaver Foundation of Greensboro is, and has been, a major benefactor of the Welfare Reform Liaison Project. As mentioned in the previous chapter, Dr. Skip Moore of the Weaver Foundation once reminded Odell that the $100,000 given to the Welfare Reform Liaison Project in 1999 was from the Weaver Foundation, not God, and Odell ought not forget that. The Weaver Foundation is very explicit about what it will not make grants for:

- Individuals
- Partisan political programs or voter registration efforts
- Conferences
- Travel or group trips
- Video productions
- Fraternal organizations
- Churches and other organizations for religious purposes

I reminded Odell that there was a message in between the lines of the phrase "a program sponsored by Mount Zion Baptist Church"—one that he would have to work hard to shake and reshape if the Welfare Reform Liaison Project were ever to become a community organization judged only by performance. The message was that the project was not yet fully part of United Way's stakeholder base, but as "part" of

Mount Zion, it was a legitimate venture for the United Way and its readership. Innocuous as such a distinction might seem, it was anything but given local history.

BLACK ICE

In my thirty years in Greensboro, a series of the city's religious nonprofits have faced serious troubles. An August 18, 1983, article in the *Greensboro Daily News* by Flontina Miller, "Salvation Army Audit Discovers Diverted Funds," reported that a local Salvation Army audit had discovered "diverted funds." Major William Williford admitted to diverting a total of $105,913 ($234,342 in purchasing power today) for personal use. The case was handled "in-house"; Williford was relieved of his position and referred to outpatient psychiatric care.

A decade later, two religious housing agencies, Greensboro Episcopal Housing Ministry, a "white"-run organization, and Project Homestead, a "black"-led non-profit housing corporation, faced intense public scrutiny for their mismanagement and financial improprieties. The only discernable difference in the intensity of the

scrutiny in the hundreds of local news articles was that Reverend Michael King, executive director of Project Homestead, was named in the headlines four times. No leader of Episcopal Housing Ministry made the headlines. Michael was an outgoing, strong, well-known community figure, shown many times in community media in his frock wearing a large visible cross. His strong presence may be

why he appeared in the headlines four times. However, in later years, rarely did the articles counterbalance what an outstanding job his organization did in getting poor people into their own homes. His organization even took over for the failed Episcopal Housing Ministry.

More recently, in 2005, when financial scandal also hit the local Habitat for Humanity, there were fewer local news articles than there were about Episcopal Housing Ministry's and Project Homestead's failings. And in Habitat's case, the offender, Sheryl Wall, was brought to court, unlike Major Williford twenty-two years earlier. She was found guilty, sentenced to a minimum of four years in prison, and ordered to pay $522,500 in restitution.

It is noteworthy that the *Greensboro News and Record*'s headline didn't name the embezzler. In its article on her sentencing, however, it did show a picture of her looking somewhat deranged. The news story also subtly took the focus off of Habitat and seemed to put the major responsibility on the culprit and her sanity, much like the 1983 article about Major Williford and the Salvation Army. Even though the judge was noted as having said that Habitat should not be completely blameless, as the organization gave her too much access to funds without controls, much of the article was subtly protecting a valuable community agency, a world-renowned faith-based organization.

Had the article been about Reverend Michael King, it is rather unlikely that coverage of the trial would've sounded like this:

> Wall, 45, wearing a pink cardigan and khaki capris, looked tired. She rocked back and forth slightly, hands clasped in front of her, as she answered the judge's questions. Her "yes, sirs" barely rose above the hum of the lights.
>
> "She's been devastated," Wall's husband, Charles "Mickey" Wall, testified. "She doesn't eat. She doesn't sleep. She sees people who aren't there. She hears voices."

At times Odell thinks that I hear voices and see things that aren't there, but he has given me the benefit of the doubt on more than one occasion and has later done a mea culpa. I have been in this community for thirty years and have closely followed how our media frames social issues overtly and subtly, like the student of community I was trained to be. A couple of years after the Williford incident in 1983, I was involved with a public history project with North Carolina Agricultural and Technical State University and University of North Carolina at Greensboro. The project was led by Dr. Bill Link of UNC Greensboro, who is white, and Dr. Bob Davis of the North Carolina A&T State University, who is black. A news article about the project pictured both leaders but referred to Bill Link as Dr. Link and referred to Dr. Davis as merely Bob Davis of North Carolina A&T. I had heard, seen, and read things in Greensboro that Odell hadn't when we met.

I told this thirtysomething newly ordained reverend, so exuberant and full of religion and religious language, that no matter how the community would define him and the Welfare Reform Liaison Project, he would have to define the agency with its performance. Performance is color blind. A religious image and language of religion, and others defining him and his organization, were not the keys to success. And it was my belief, and still is, that one misstep and he and his organization would be inextricably bound in a racial story—unlike Salvation Army, Episcopal Housing Ministry's, Habitat for Humanity, and other "white" organizations.

When Greensboro Urban Ministry holds its CROP Walk for the Hungry, the five thousand walkers don't walk for Reverend Mike Aiken, the agency leader. Sure, the walkers may have been spurred on by their own religious leaders who were "hugged" by Mike Aiken. But the community chatter created by those walkers going door-to-door to solicit sponsors to help the organization with its mission made the community own the organization and its cause.

THE MANTRA: PERFORMANCE

Major Williford, not the Salvation Army, was crazy. Sheryl Wall heard voices, but Habitat for Humanity didn't. The only way for the Welfare Reform Liaison Project to avoid slipping on black ice in the public's eye and avoid race and the black church being perceived as a failure was, from my view, to create a community organization that had a reputation for unblemished performance that would live beyond its first leader and its founding church. I told Odell over and over and over that the Welfare Reform Liaison Project has to be from Mount Zion, not of Mount Zion. Sometimes, especially in basketball, learning, or performance, is a function of time and repetition, and I repeated this mantra to Odell all the time.

ODELL GOT IT

I harped on Odell a lot during those early days, but it wasn't until early 2001 that I became convinced he truly understood that the Welfare Reform Liaison Project had to be from the church, not of it. In April of that year, we participated in daylong conference in Raleigh, North Carolina, hosted by the American Family Coalition. The conference focused on President Bush's new faith-based initiative. There was even a live satellite hookup directly to Washington, and more than fifty cities were participating in the conference. We witnessed live the introduction of HR7, a congressional bill designed to expand activities that promote more Christ-centered religion in federal programs, thus broadening Bush's faith-based initiatives.

Odell couldn't stomach my skepticism of Bush's initiative until that day, but deep down, he thought that because I was Jewish and I didn't drink from the Christian troth, I simply didn't get it. He thought that I was just crazy with my rants that the initiative could not work because it was targeting black churches—little ones who had no mentoring and zero knowledge of how to play in the community culture of interlocking partnerships.

It was different in 2001. Our trust wasn't as deep as it is today, but we had enough trust for him to listen until he learned the game. My footprint is on just about every one of the grants that came into the Welfare Reform Liaison Project up until that time, and because I received no money for the help I provided, he trusted me with money matters. Matters of faith, though, were an entirely different matter.

The carefully scripted event in Washington that day, which we watched from Raleigh, had the feel and all the trappings of a presidential convention—live entertainment, dignitaries, and politicians marching to the podium, one after another, to praise Bush's faith-based initiatives and the power of faith in service delivery.

I was astonished earlier that morning to discover that the American Family Coalition, the host of the conference, was a front for the Unification Church. The "Moonies" were running the show. Both Odell and I grew further astounded as we listened to participants, mostly from small black churches, read and discuss meditations of Reverend Sun Myung Moon. Still more amazing to me was the discovery that the Washington Times Foundation, Moon's organization, funded the satellite hookups. We quickly realized that Bush's initiative was desperate but very serious about getting the black churches under its white policy umbrella. This was neither a joke nor a hallucination—even though I was spinning out of control inside. It was real, serious, and scary to me from the moment I walked into the conference event.

Odell and I had talked frequently about what it means to be a minority in American society, but until that morning, he had never quite understood how someone like me, a non-Christian white person, could feel out of place in America. My friend Odell had an epiphany when he realized that, throughout much of the morning session, he witnessed me quiet as a stone and pale.

All morning I was excluded from a faith-based initiative that was touted as inclusive in its public proclamations but that would not let me into its carefully choreographed country club. And it was by design. Small black churches and ministries like Odell's were carefully mined and personally invited to the event. Odell called and asked whether he could bring a guest and was told he could, which is why I, a good Jewish liberal, made it into the event.

During a break, when we were off in a corner, Odell looked me straight in the eye and said, "I am a born-again black Baptist preacher, but now I know what it feels like to be a Jew!" Over the years, Odell often was the only black professional in business meetings, so he knew what it felt like to be in a room full of white people and be to talked over and around, as if he and his opinions didn't exist or matter. As a black, born-again Christian preacher sitting next to "his invited Jewish friend, coach and mentor," Odell realized that his friend was in a room of Christians and was being talked over and around as if he or his religion didn't exist. He saw the sadness in my eyes. It was his utterance that convinced me that Odell would succeed in the community. But it was our burgeoning friendship and growing love for each other that kept him listening and following my behind-the-scenes tutelage, even though we disagreed, and still do, until he finally understood in his soul what I was talking about. When you are of the church you can be exclusive and exclude or be excluded—when you are from the church in the community's common space, of and for the community come first. The thin trust Odell had for me after we won the smoke-and-mirrors grant kept him slowly but surely hanging on to what I was saying over and over: he would get nailed if he failed. He was a black, exuberant reverend with a new idea and a new program, but he had to win the trust of the community because others, both black and white, had lost some of that trust before he ever arrived on the scene. A new kid on the block—a talented professional who picked and chose if or how he would use what I put forth, and someone who played the game and did well—was embroiled in a solid stew of social constraints of which he was only slowly becoming aware.

There were four agencies in the community that were larger than life when we started out: Greensboro Urban Ministry, Triad Health Project, Hospice of Greater Greensboro, and Family and Children's Services of the Piedmont. The agencies had one thing in common: they were perceived as belonging to the whole community. Those agencies brought the entire community together in common cause around the issues they each addressed. Greensboro Urban Ministry managed poverty and its corollaries: homelessness and hunger. Family and Children's Services of the Piedmont led the institutional response to rape, family violence, child protection, and general family well-being. Triad Health Project brought the community together around HIV and AIDS, and Hospice of Greater Greensboro was the primary provider of palliative care.

The Welfare Reform Liaison Project had to bring the community together around workforce development, first by putting welfare recipients to work and making sure they succeeded and then by succeeding on the backside of workforce development, including the development of an institutional volunteer corps. It had to put the difficult to employ—ex-prisoners, people with disabilities, and new documented immigrants—into the workforce and keep them working.

Doing so was going to be an enormous challenge. And getting funders and partners to sign on when it was hardly clear the challenge could be met—that would take quite a bit of convincing, something that could happen only when Odell carefully and deliberately chose every single word he uttered.

I gave Odell a set of talking points to use in his community discussions after the Welfare Reform Liaison Project had opened its doors (see box on page 82). The talking points suggest how to present the agency in the community and how to talk to the media, which by then was shaping the story of the project in its own way. We did not want to be bystanders in the community story line. We needed to shape it, too.

This was another of the social constraints, according to Jim Collins, that organizations in community life regularly face. Odell and I talked often about who would shape the organization's future and tried to manage the story the best we could. The community had to think of the Welfare Reform Liaison Project as an agency with which other agencies wanted to be in partnership. Odell had to be able to talk about

---

Talking Points

July 15, 1999

Please memorize the following script.

From the beginning, Welfare Reform Liaison Project has been in a PARTNER-
SHIP trying to help women and children make decent lives as they move
from welfare to work. To be successful, we needed a new approach to
addressing the COMPLEX problems associated with welfare. Welfare is not
just about a person's individual will to succeed. It is also about CHILD CARE,
it is about HEALTH AND HOUSING and TRANSPORTATION. It is about earning enough money to NURTURE a family. It is about UNDERSTANDING on the
part of the employer and community. It is about LINKING the array of services to meet the needs of our clients. Since our clients are different, the
configuration of the support services they need to keep them EMPLOYED are
different. We have the support of the church but we are NOT THE CHURCH.
Welfare reform liaison project is not just a new program it is a NEW WAY to
approach solving community problems. We see ourselves as PUBLIC SAMAR-
ITANS, WHO EXPRESS THEIR FAITH BY taking leadership in helping the
Partnership Help Women and Children.

---

the complex problems participants in his program faced, in simple language—about
barriers that kept them from obtaining work and thus hindered the nurturing of
their families successfully. Without a doubt, the barriers were many. Lack of housing, inadequate child care, and inadequate transportation are often systemic problems that bear heavily on people who feel they can hurdle the barricades. To overcome the Cadillac-driving stigma toward welfare recipients, we needed to educate the
community regularly.

MAKING THE CASE WITH A MAP

I asked Odell whether he would contact the city planning department for help in
developing a GPS map showing where the welfare recipients were living in the community, where the churches were that were likely to have day-care centers, where
the bus lines ran, where the city limits extended, where the white churches that
often helped were located, and where the jobs were located. Odell printed up a
poster-size version of that map (figure 6). With that map in hand, he usually didn't
need to explain much to a community audience about how difficult it was for

welfare recipients to get a bus to get their children to day care, get a transfer to then get to work, and often to have to make personal arrangements to get to the final destination because the bus lines ended before they reached the places where the new jobs were being developed, close to the airport.

This methodology worked very well when Odell spoke to the business community. At the local level, it is easier to have a discussion about welfare to work with some graphics that display the facts about barriers than it is at the national level, where one must chip away at years of myths and stereotypes.

It should be pointed out that state and local leaders understood that regional economic development was intricately connected to a mobile workforce and had been planning a regional transportation system not just to transport workers to where the new jobs were located in Greensboro or the surrounding county but also to move people efficiently throughout the region by developing a comprehensive regional transportation system. That operation did not begin until 2002. The new welfare reform policy and attending transportation problems its workforce participants faced, however, went into effect in 1997, leaving the entire system of welfare-to-

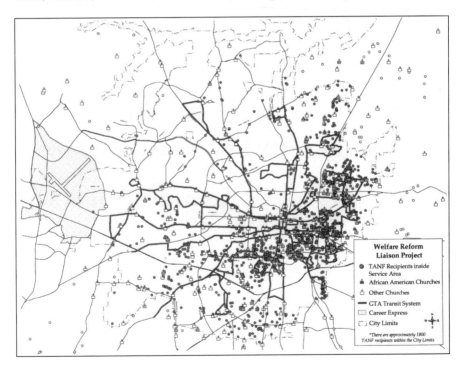

FIGURE 6. *Welfare Reform Liaison Project*

work participants and employers to their own devices to transport people who had no cars or connecting bus lines to get to a job.

A key feature of the current system, Piedmont Authority Regional Transportation (PART), is Part Express, which gets people to jobs around the airport. The chatter that we and many other groups created in the community led to the Emergency Ride Home program. Emergency Ride Home provides participants—commuters who regularly ride the bus, carpool, bike, or walk—with a reliable ride home on days the person has used an alternative mode of transportation to get to work. This concern was one that kept an able workforce from seeking and maintaining employment in areas where they could not get home for an emergency.

The results of our work might not have been fancy, but they were actually helping people who truly needed help—these were thorny situations that demanded action rather than pontification.

We faced women with hungry children who were required to work but had no way to get to a job, ex-prisoners who more likely than not would return to jail without steady employment, people with disabilities, immigrants—in other words, the most difficult in society to employ. That pool of people did not have the best chance of making it if we didn't get things right, and right from the beginning.

We had to keep getting it right in what was a long race to being viewed as larger than life in the local social services community. We strived to produce results that the community could see and be a part of, too.

Organizations in the community that consciously race for recognition are like any other kind of racer, and the Welfare Reform Liaison Project was no different. There are benefits to be gained by being in the tailwinds of leaders. The smart racers use the energy of the leaders to reduce the resistance of facing headwinds straight on.

In community action, sometimes the tailwinds are controllable, and sometimes they are not. Performance, however, is controllable—and Odell has kept his eye on the larger mission of helping people, each and every minute. He has performed well, again and again, and it is that well-earned reputation for reliable performance that has made the Welfare Reform Liaison Project the nationally recognized workforce development organization that it is today and a step closer to the color of water—the black ice is melting.

CHAPTER 7

The Golden Egg

Nonprofit organizations need several funding streams to ensure viability and meet payroll if something goes wrong. There is nothing more comforting than a stable funding source. When I was a doctoral student, my policy professor, Roy Lubove, used to remind us that the goose that laid the golden egg was business. I reminded Odell that he would be permanently successful if he had a business venture. Little did we know how correct Professor Lubove was. But it took our making connections for that gold to glitter.

A CONFIDANT

Even before the big money started to roll in—and it did, with numerous small grants flowing in to the Welfare Reform Liaison Project and then two back-to-back state grants of $212,000 in 2001 and 2002—I kept telling Odell that the goose that lays the golden egg is not grant money, especially government grant money, but stable funding.

Odell had to come up with that golden egg or the early winning efforts would turn to losses as soon as a new community issue was hotter than welfare reform. A shift in a community's philanthropic and public dollars can turn on a dime if, for example, someone is murdered in a gang attack or a child in foster care goes missing. Grant money is good, and it is necessary, but it is never sufficient.

Odell agreed that the grant game was hard work and could be short lived, especially if the winds of social policy shifted. In recent years, Odell has given many speeches on social entrepreneurism—the efforts that go into developing the stable funding base—and I have attended some of them. He rocks the audience.

But thirteen years ago, back in the days of our conversations about stabilized funding, Odell thought he simply needed to hustle to create a steady stream of income. He went about it as he had done on the way to becoming a top salesman nationally for his trucking and logistics firm: by building a strong customer base.

Independent of all my banter about stable funding, I felt that Odell ought to have an insider in the United Way as a confidant. A former student of mine, Nathan Cook, was working at the United Way. Nathan had transferred to our social work program from a small Bible college in Alabama when I was a young assistant professor, and I was assigned to be his adviser. Nathan came into my office for me to help him map out his course schedule. He had a poor academic record.

In our conversation, I found out that he was a black belt in karate. As a former athlete, I knew the amount of time Nathan had to put into karate to become a master. Being much more brazen and far less measured in my younger days than I am now in my more golden years, I looked Nathan in the eye and said that I expected him to work as hard at school as he did at karate.

Nathan has been a devoutly religious man since I have known him, but as he tells it (with a big grin on his face), when I confronted him with that challenge, he wanted to kill me on the spot. He said it took every fiber in his body to hold himself back.

Nathan went on to become one of my finer students and a good friend, but not without going through some ringers, especially in my grant-writing class, where I bloodied his work like I did Odell's drafts of our smoke-and-mirrors grant. He became a mainstay in Greensboro's social service community, working his way up to be a vice president in the United Way.

I invited Odell and Nathan to lunch at Elizabeth's Pizza in Greensboro. That day Odell ended up being served a dish far better than a regular slice: a golden egg, courtesy of Nathan Cook.

GIFTS IN KIND

At the time of our pizza meeting, Nathan was overseeing the Gifts in Kind program at the United Way. Gifts in Kind International is a foundation that at the time had a business model to work with corporations to ensure that they donated stockpiled goods to nonprofit organizations, mainly through the United Way's national network of 1,485 organizations. If a company like Kmart had new goods that were unsellable for some reason—a tear in some plastic packaging, say, or out-of-style clothing—the company would have to move those goods off the floor and into warehouses. But those goods take up space needed for new products. So it is in the fiscal interest of corporations to move them as quickly as possible.

A United Way organization seeking goods for its nonprofits could ship a load of donated goods very cheaply and then turn around and distribute the goods to local nonprofits. Little money exchanged hands. This process was nice in theory, but United Ways are not warehousers or distributors, so the program didn't have the infrastructure that provided real benefits, a real zing, to communities. Odell, though, knew all about both trucking and warehousing.

As Nathan was telling Odell how the system worked over lunch, he noted that if a nonprofit received a shipment of goods and had excess goods left over, it could not sell them outright, but it could charge an administration fee to redistribute them to other nonprofits that could use the goods. When Odell heard that, he became very fidgety during lunch and left sooner than expected.

I thought the connection with Nathan bombed, but it was quite to the contrary. It was at Elizabeth's Pizza, in the Lawndale Shopping Plaza in Greensboro, that the trucking expert and visionary Odell Cleveland found his golden opportunity. He knew that the tiny loophole in the policy—the one that allowed nonprofits with excess donations to recoup administrative fees for redistribution if the organization did not need the goods—was the golden egg that would enable him to order many truck-loads of goods, teach his students work habits by having them sort the goods, and have enough bulk left over to make enough money to put back into the training efforts. He would do this by charging a small administrative fee to churches and organizations that served low-income people for the goods they purchased at what would become the Job Training Distribution Center's retail outlet.

Odell envisioned the Welfare Reform Liaison Project making money by developing a nonprofit Sam's Club–like operation, enough to pay stipends to students, some of whom would then have their first complete work experience on their résumé. Odell is not the type to ramble on about an idea, especially when it is between God and him. He saw the light, which beamed in on something that few saw.

THE DISTRIBUTION CENTER IS BORN

Before I had a clue what he was talking about in late 1998, the first truckload of clothing arrived at the Annex, across from Mount Zion. I still remember Angelia

Ijames, whom we talked about in chapter 2, sorting a load of clothes in the garage attached to the Annex. But before I even grasped what Odell was up to, he was moving like a stallion in an open range, quickly and gracefully, as if nothing were in his way—as he often does when an idea hits him.

The distribution training aspect of the program was moving to a sixteen-thousand-square-foot space across from Greensboro Urban Ministry and the Salvation Army retail store. The intake, case management, computer training, and other program parts stayed at the Annex. Odell loved the new space, but he hated the location. He didn't want to be branded as a "welfare organization" by location alone, given the project's proximity to other charities. He felt he was in the center of the human service culture, but he was training people for business, and he wanted to instill a business mentality, which being entangled in the human services system confounded.

Gifts in Kind Wins Top National Award

The Gifts in Kind program received the 2000 Pinnacle Award, the highest honor given by Gifts in Kind International. Gifts in Kind programs distribute goods, received primarily from businesses, to local nonprofits to help those in need.

The Greensboro program is now the largest in the nation, growing from $6 million in inventory in 1999, its first full year of operation, to $14 million in inventory in 2000. Sacramento, California, with $7 million, is the second largest program.

"When you add $14 million from Gifts in Kind to the annual campaign and grants, United Way is bringing more than $30 million in annual resources into the Greater Greensboro community," Neil Belenky, President of United Way said.

Nathan Cook, Vice President of Community Initiatives, attributes the growth of the local program to its partnership with the Welfare Reform Liaison Program, a ministry of Mt. Zion Baptist Church. WRLP opened a warehouse and training facility in May that distributes the inventory.

Odell Cleveland, Executive Director of WRLP, said what makes Gifts in Kind rewarding is the opportunity to help families rebuild their lives. "When someone leaves an abusive spouse with nothing but the clothes on their back and their children in their arms, we can put together what they need." By customizing an order of new clothing, shoes, household appliances, personal care items and more, Gifts in Kind can start to restore what someone has lost, he said. Victims of fires are another group Gifts in Kind helps start over again. Cleveland said Gifts in Kind had helped more than 25,000 individuals in 2000.

To participate, a Greater Greensboro nonprofit organization 501(c)(3) must register, pay a $150 registration fee for two years, and then pay a token administrative fee for goods they receive. Currently, only 38 organizations are registered. Among the companies who donate goods are Sears, Avon, Nine West, Sara Lee and Office Depot. ∎

Nathan Cook, Vice President of Community Services and the Pinnacle Award.

FIGURE 7

Given Odell's concerns, one might reasonably ask why he still keeps the name Welfare Reform Liaison Project for his agency, given how long ago Clinton's welfare reforms seem to have occurred. As always, Odell is ready with an answer. From the first day, inspired by a passage in the book of Numbers, Odell believed that he was going to reform welfare in Greensboro by creating liaisons between his clientele and business. He created a distribution training center to accomplish the change. And when badgered to change the name, as has happened many times, he confidently says that welfare is "well-being" and that he is reforming the way welfare has been brought to low-income people—end of discussion.

When one walks into the project's current operation for the first time, its corporate atmosphere is initially shocking. And yet the first picture one sees on a table of important photos is Odell's first case-management team. To this day, Odell sings their praises for giving the organization the reputation of caring for its patrons and providing service differently than public welfare service providers in both spirit and practice. The spirit of those caseworkers rings throughout the program today, even as the program has grown and changed. Odell doesn't, as he often says, "forget who brought him to the dance."

Knowing Odell like I do now, I know he had plans in mind for a bigger, more businesslike atmosphere the day he moved part of the operations from the church-owned Annex to the first big warehouse distribution center off of Lee Street in Greensboro. More and more trucks arrived at the warehouse on Lee Street, and Odell started to work his magic in partnering with the United Way and Nathan Cook to start mass distribution of goods that poor people could afford and to do so through nonprofit and congregational memberships, which would allow for bulk and eventually individual purchases through a membership system.

Recognition of Odell's accomplishments came far more quickly than either of us could have imagined. A *Greensboro News and Record* clipping (figure 7), from August 1999, reports on the federal Department of Housing and Urban Development's naming of the Welfare Reform Liaison Project as "one of the 200 best community practices in the nation."

AWARDS CAME FAST, AND SO DID LEGITIMACY

Earning national recognition a year and a half after winning the smoke-and-mirrors grant was an exceptional feat. The project that won the Welfare Reform Liaison Project the award was a joint effort with the United Way and the Department of Housing and Urban Development (HUD) (figure 8).

The plan was to have the Welfare Reform Liaison Project and the United Way's Gifts in Kind efforts work with Greensboro Housing Authority personnel and small neighborhood churches to distribute goods to the residents of Greensboro's largest housing project. The trucking expert had no problem routing loads of goods from different corporate warehouses to his center. The project was a smashing success on every level imaginable, with HUD giving out two hundred awards to 3,200 eligible recipients that year.

The U.S. Department of Housing and Urban Development recently named the program one of the 200 best community building practices in the nation. The program provides two major services to Guilford County: It is a job training opportunity for people who are in the Work First (Welfare) program and for individuals living in poverty, and it provides new merchandise such as clothing, computers, personal care products and paper products to agencies and churches that provide direct services to families. At the Welfare Reform Liaison Project Distribution Training Center on Alamance Church Road, men and women learn many of the skills necessary to break free of welfare. They also get information, encouragement and inspiration to help them take steps forward in their lives. The project is the work of the Rev. Odell Cleveland and the get-it-done philosophy of Mt. Zion Church, where Cleveland is an associate minister. The United Way, through its Gifts in Kind International program, brings into the program inventory and free merchandise ranging from clothing to computer software. *News & Record (Greensboro, NC) 8/22/1999*

Recognized as one of the "Best Practice in Housing and Community Development" prigrams in the nation by US Department of Housing and Urban Development.
Left to Right: Rev. Odell Cleveland, Executive Director of WRLP. Mr. Davie, Regional Representative from HUD, Nathan Cook, Vice-President of United Way of Greater Greenboro

FIGURE 8. *Winning the HUD Award*

Although nationally the United Way's Gifts in Kind program was languishing, in Greensboro it was beginning to grow vigorously, and because of Odell's contacts and know-how in the trucking industry. He peered through a tiny loophole in the Gifts in Kind policy and saw truckloads of goods pouring into Greensboro, along with millions of dollars of new but unused corporate goods waiting to be unloaded, separated, and distributed by a "workforce in training." He saw his market as neighborhood churches trying to enhance their outreach ministries in ways that could reduce financial burdens on the already financially burdened working poor. Some of the poor happened to be women who were on welfare, women who had been tossed with little training and without workforce habits into a reckless and dynamic marketplace. Odell was going to shape their habits as the first step on the ladder to employment success—with the soul and vigor of your stereotypical born-again black Baptist preacher and Stephen Covey's training under his belt.

Word got out fast in the neighborhood that the Welfare Reform Liaison Project was really there to help. And the tone of the news article regarding the church connection improved slightly, so we were thrilled to be moving the story line in what we thought was the direction of being from the church and not of the church.

Good things were happening fast. Two days after the article was published, on August 24, 1999, Odell received an award letter from the Weaver Foundation in Greensboro, which granted him $100,000 to expand his warehousing and distribution efforts (figure 9).

The Weaver family was an early leader in breaking down barriers of segregation in the construction industry and in Greensboro's white business community. Mike Weaver and his wife, Catherine Stern, are leading philanthropists and highly regarded businesspeople in the Greensboro community. They approach nonprofit development in the way that venture capitalists seek out innovators and provide start-up capital and ensure that the venture succeeds by keeping a close eye on project development, by giving a shot in the arm when the venture is moving increasingly toward success, and by stepping in to help guide when things move off course.

The Weaver Foundation's president, Dr. Skip Moore, a university colleague of mine for close to fifteen years before he moved to this position at the foundation, does not accept unsolicited proposals. He and his staff keep their ears to the ground and eyes on the lookout, seeking out promising ventures like they did with the Welfare Reform Liaison Project. On my wall in the "man cave," my basement office where Odell and I have met for quiet, uninterrupted, and serious matters regarding

the development of this program on and off for thirteen years, is a sign that reads: "Ribbon Cutting Ceremony, May 4, 8:30–9:30." That red, white, and blue ribbon hangs from the sign as a memento of the official opening of the second of four distribution centers Odell has built so

From left to right: Mike Weaver, Weaver Foundation; Neil Belenky, United Way of Greater Greensboro; Phyllis Jones, Welfare Reform Liaison Project; and Bishop George W. Brooks, Mount Zion Baptist Church

August 24, 1999

Rev. Odell Cleveland
Welfare Reform Liaison Project, Inc.
1324 Alamance Church Road
Greensboro, NC 27406

Dear Rev. Cleveland:

I am writing on behalf of the Board of Directors of the Weaver Foundation to confirm our grant to your organization of $100,000, payable over three years. The purpose of this grant is to assist you in securing and operating a warehouse as a training/office site for the Project. The grant will provide $40,000 in the first year with $30,000 available for rent, utilities, and related expenses plus $10,000 for shelving, equipment, furnishings, and relocation expense. We will provide $30,000 in each of the next two years to cover rent, utilities, and related expenses.

Jim Rucker, of South Atlantic Warehouse Corporation, has agreed to work with you on a volunteer basis to help you locate a suitable facility and to negotiate a contract. His company may have a suitable warehouse for your use or he may be able to help you find one. His phone number is 379-0971 and his address is: PO Drawer 730, Greensboro 27402.

Please review the attached grant agreement. Sign and return the original to indicate your acceptance of its terms and conditions. I look forward to working with you as your program grows in the next few years.

Best wishes.

Sincerely,

Richard L. Moore
President

RLM/ms
WEAVER FOUNDATION, INC.
POST OFFICE BOX 16030
GREENSBORO, NORTH CAROLINA
27416-0030
(336) 275-9222

FIGURE 9.

far. The opening took place nine months after the Weaver Foundation's grant money came in.

On a very real level, that ribbon-cutting picture shows that we were moving in the direction of community ownership, of being owned by the community in a symbolic, partnering, and financial sense. It seemed as if we were beginning to be

American Express	1999	$ 14,500.00	
Catholic Campaign	1999	$ 1,200.00	
Cemala Foundation	1998	$ 25,000.00	
	1999	$ 25,000.00	
	2000	$ 46,800.00	$ 96,800.00
Community Foundation	1998	$ 10,000.00	
	1999	$ 10,000.00	
	2001	$ 4,000.00	$ 24,000.00
D. Michael Warner Foundation	1999	$ 15,000.00	
Gannett Foundation	2000	$ 500.00	
Jefferson Pilot	1999	$ 5,000.00	
Joseph M. Bryant Foundation	1998	$ 25,000.00	
	2000	$ 39,000.00	
	2001	$ 21,000.00	$ 85,000.00
Kathleen & Joseph M. Bryan Foundation	1999	$ 19,000.00	
	2000	$ 20,000.00	
	2001	$ 19,000.00	$ 58,000.00
Kathleen Price Bryan Family Fund	1998	$ 25,000.00	
Mary Norris Preyer Foundation	2000	$ 6,000.00	
	2001	$ 6,000.00	$ 12,000.00
Moses Cone–Wesley Long Foundation	1999	$ 21,000.00	
	2000	$ 21,000.00	
	2001	$ 2,000.00	$ 44,000.00
Mount Zion Baptist Church	1999	$ 50,000.00	
	2000	$ 50,000.00	
	2001	$ 50,000.00	$ 150,000.00
NC Dept. of Health & Human Services	2000	$ 212,050.00	
	2001	$ 212,050.00	$ 424,100.00

FIGURE 10. *1998–2001 Grants, Contributions, and Other Revenues*

perceived clearly as from the church. But then just look at Bishop Brooks of Mount Zion in the picture. He is peering out as if he were overseeing the cutting while holding the ribbon tightly as Mike Weaver of the Weaver Foundation gets a clean cut. The bishop doesn't want the Welfare Relief Liaison Project to ever lose its spiritual underpinnings. But the picture suggests that the Welfare Reform Liaison Project is from Mount Zion but now belongs to the community too.

Even so, ribbons and words are not the same. I harped at Odell about being of the church and from the church, an issue that would get a bit more straightened out when Fred Newman became part of the organization (we discuss Fred in detail later on).

Money was rolling in, as a partial listing of grants in figure 10 illustrates. With the help of a partnership with the United Way, local, communitywide news stories about the program's success, and a reduction of the sixteen-week training program to twelve weeks, which increased the number of students in the program over the year, things could not seem better externally or more balanced internally.

ODELL IGNORED ME

But there were still real problems. Odell wasn't talking publicly the way I had outlined for him in the talking points. Not only was he talking about God to the community at large, but also he was sounding too preachy for my tastes, and his preachiness seemed indiscriminate.

I warned him over and over about using that ladder of abstraction carefully. I believed that, in the short run, the kind of community voice he was speaking with in the newspaper worked very well. It also sustained Odell's successes and fantastically reinforced him, despite my regular warnings that the turtle won the race.

He was moving a bit too fast for me with all that money pouring in, and he still was speaking publicly to an exclusive audience. And he knew it—to this day, he remains convinced that it was the right way to go.

"Do you think that Dr. Alvin and Tracey Powell [of Mount Zion Baptist Church] would have donated $5,000 if the program wasn't anointed?" he asked me recently. "Do you think I would have the support of some of the people who may not care less about welfare recipients if I didn't talk about a hand up not a hand out, about pity parties? Growing up in South Carolina I was taught that blacks will have to be twice as good to get credit for doing a good job. No, it's not fair, but it's life."

Thirteen years later, I now realize that we were walking a tightrope of local politics in its raw form—something we often privately called the fingernail dirt of local community development.

A STEP BACK INTO OUR PRIVATE WORLD

A momentary diversion is in order here. Race in America is complex even when best friends of different races are talking about it. Imagine for a moment what our private conversations must be like when we know that people in our own community—black and white, Christian and non-Christian—will read and scrutinize this story.

I wanted to present the matters in the last chapter of this book from my perch exclusively, as I have strong opinions formed from my careful study of this human service community. Odell did not like my first approach. And as we sat together and he read the first draft, he asked this simple but profound question: "How have white-run faith-based agencies been portrayed in the press over the years? You can't even imply that Michael King's Project Homestead was treated differently unless you have some evidence." I listened and then spent three days hunting down all the local articles that were pertinent to what turned out to be two pages of narrative to get it right for both of us. Odell's query jolted my memory back to the 1980s, when there was no Internet and I kept every local story and hunted down numerous national stories of faith-based social services, catalogued at the time on microfiche. LexisNexis catalogs our local stories only from 1990 onward, and my print news folder from twenty-five years ago is gone. So there I was in a time warp in the library hunting down something that may have been a figment of my imagination (I am, after all, moving on into my golden years). I eventually found the article, but so what? What was I going to do with it?

I had writer's block, the writer's equivalent of catatonia—I could not get a word out! The reason: no matter how I thought about writing about race, someone in Greensboro would take issue—just like Odell and I took issue with each other over God anointing his program and the fact that he wasn't running a pity party. We both had it right—but Odell had it more right—and we both had it wrong.

For those readers in Greensboro, all we ask is that you remember that we struggled to respectfully get the story right, including getting it right for each other, knowing full well that some will find it dead wrong and to others it will be a bull's eye. Talking about race is like being on two different sides of the globe talking about the sun. On one side it is going down, and on the other it is rising.

IMPORTANCE OF EDUCATING THE COMMUNITY

I use the fable of the hare and the tortoise in my teaching. I shortened it with Odell with respect to program planning because it is an easy framework for making the point that there are so many little things that have to be put in place to make a program work, that going too fast out of the starting gate tires out an organization because of all the backtracking that must be done to fix what was missed when the organization was moving at great speed or out of control. Educating the community isn't at the top of lists in program development books, but it always has been a top vote getter in my framework.

Odell was educating the community—sadly, it seemed to me, like a prisoner of his own naïveté. And I was arguing with him about the sun from the opposite side of the earth. We now both agree that, over the long haul, the community needed sustained education, so when the words *Welfare Reform Liaison Project* came up, regardless of venue, they would evoke similar sentiments about what a good organization it was and whether someone from the low-income community or business community was listening.

Back in 1999, Odell played to the cheerleaders of the common but incorrect and not-so-sober welfare narrative. In my view, he needed to take the higher ground if he wanted to be a larger-than-life workforce development leader in Greensboro.

I have worked with numerous agencies in my thirty-year university career, and I have met many people whose vision and deep commitment to fix a vexing social problem by developing a nonprofit organization were so out of balance with the things that needed to be done to make their dream a reality. They failed outright or developed programs that limped along and struggled year in and year out. It is so terribly difficult for extremely passionate people to imagine things beyond what is driving their passion.

A good board of directors often means no more than just their friends' names on a form, not a key piece in an intricate organizational puzzle. A needs assessment is a foreigner who doesn't speak to their heartfelt and all encompassing urgency. Money and passion can tackle the problem that concerns them.

I have seen board members nod off when I dig deep into the details about the complexity of the problem they want to solve, and I have watched them stare blankly when I note that they need community partners who are or need to be educated about what they want to accomplish over the long term. They have no conception that they will inevitably be working with an array of unimagined people and institutions to make their dreams a reality. And they look like I am speaking gibberish when I tell them that they have to know how to speak publicly about their issue and program. I say, "All eyes are watching"—and a decade ago that is exactly what they were doing with Odell's Welfare Reform Liaison Project.

ALL EYES ARE WATCHING

Our community strategy was working, despite my consternation with Odell's ministerial exuberance and his thinking that I was out of touch with the black church. In a small town, the human services network is an interlocking one in which good news and bad news travel at the speed of the moccasin telegraph of old and the "tweet" of today. By late 1999, the Welfare Reform Liaison Project and Odell were receiving a considerable amount of public media attention as the Gifts in Kind goods from corporate America's warehouses were rolling in and doing more good than anyone but Odell Cleveland had imagined.

If there were any doubts left in Odell's mind that there are eyes all over watching, they were laid to rest by a letter from Samantha Ibarguen, of Merrill Lynch in New York, in November 2000 (figure 11).

The Pratt Family Foundation of Greensboro created a small foundation to help with the social good in our community and Merrill Lynch held the foundation's assets. This is not an uncommon practice for people who want to use some of their private assets to help their communities. In fact, it is part of the American fabric of private philanthropy. Many of these charities don't have public requests for proposals. The leaders of such foundations would much prefer to invite organizations they deem worthy to submit a proposal.

Family foundations that operate this way are always on the lookout for promising

 **Merrill Lynch**

Samantha Ibarguen
Philanthropy Research Analyst

Merrill Lynch Trust Company
Family Office Group
2 World Financial Center, Floor 38
New York, NY 10281-6100
212-236-1554
FAX 212-236-5936

November 9, 2000

Reverend Odell Cleveland
Welfare Reform Liaison Project, Inc.
1324 Alamance Church Road
Greensboro, NC 27406

Dear Rev. Cleveland,

   I am writing on behalf of a private Family Foundation that has expressed interest in Welfare Reform Liaison Project. This Family Foundation, located in the Piedmont area, is eager to work with a select number of non-profits to increase funding for causes such as family support and welfare. In order to do so most effectively, the Foundation has established a grant program so that its funds may benefit the community in a structured and purposeful manner.

   We have briefly reviewed your organization and are interested in the work you do for the community. We would like to be able to learn more about your programs, including the extent of your outreach in the Piedmont, as well as the goals and needs of WRLP for the year 2001.

   If you are interested becoming eligible for grants ranging from $5,000 to $25,000 from this Foundation, please submit information related to the above inquiries to the following address:
        Samantha Ibarguen
        Merrill Lynch
        2 World Financial Center, 38th Floor
        New York, NY 10281

   Upon reviewing your response, the Family Foundation will begin working closely with those organizations it feels can best benefit the community based upon its priorities.

Sincerely,

Samantha Ibarguen
Samantha Ibarguen

FIGURE 11.

uses for their philanthropic dollars. And leaders of organizations who know that there are stakeholders in the community who may not be in their network or visible in their scope of potential funders need to be very aware of what they say and do in public, and what is said about them. Someone is always watching, and sometimes that someone has a checkbook in hand, as this excerpt from Samantha Ibarguen's letters attests: "We have briefly reviewed your organization and are interested in the work you do for the community. We would like to be able to learn more about your programs, including the extent of your outreach in the Piedmont, as well as the goals and needs of WRLP for the year 2001."

Without a doubt, Odell was on a roll with the grants.

CHAPTER 8

Playing the Grant Game

An agency can sustain itself on one- and two-year grants for just so long. Given the free market private funding world, an exciting new program becomes less so and more routine after a couple of years. So even stable agencies must innovate, or give the appearance of innovation, so that their brand looks new to funders. This worried me. Welfare Reform Liaison Project needed a long-term stable funding base.

There is no question for Odell that with each grant that rolled into the agency—whether or not we sweated long hours and bled red ink, whether the money was a gift from God or a gift from the Weaver Foundation—the Italian lunch at Elizabeth's Pizza was nothing less than the hand of God at work.

I, nor any earthly being, will ever convince him otherwise. Odell maneuvered his way into a strong personal friendship with Nathan Cook of the United Way. He became a real buddy with the United Way's president, Neil Belenky, and he worked very closely with him on numerous community projects. And he ended up with Fred Newman of the United Way working daily beside him over the past seven years. Odell's membership on the finance committee of the United Way is no accident either—no matter whether we frame the events in this book as a set of well-thought-out moves on a community chessboard, my take on developments, or simply attribute all the things moved around on the chess board to God's hand, which is Odell's view of things. Odell's heart knows the answer. I am sticking with hard work—and with realizing what is opportunity and what isn't. Divine intervention or not, from the beginning, the United Way increasingly saw an opportunity in partnering with the Welfare Reform Liaison Project and Reverend Odell Cleveland. As the 2001 *Your Way* newsletter reports, within eighteen months of that lunch at Elizabeth's Pizza, not only had Odell received state and national awards, so had Nathan Cook and the United Way (see figure 7 in the previous chapter).

IN BETWEEN THE LINES

Three paragraphs in the *Your Way* story are much more significant than they appear on first read. Those lines tie into a lifetime of community politics about what went on behind the scenes. What went on in between those lines is instructive not only because it points to the increasingly intricate relationship that was taking place between the Welfare Reform Liaison Project and the United Way in Greensboro but also because such relationships have been and continue to be forged in communities everywhere. United Way was blowing a message to the broader community about race relations, about leveraging the social capital in tenuous partnerships, about broad-based community legitimacy, about what signifies success in Greensboro, and about how putting a local community on the state and national radar is also about winning. Those winds raised the tides to lift all boats.

HISTORICAL PERSPECTIVE

Perhaps a bit of historical perspective is helpful here, including a rarely discussed but important issue in the United Way's funding world. The United Way of Denver's Web site contains a brief history of the organization, as the network of 1,485 United Ways began in Denver:

> The first United Way was founded right here in Denver, Colorado, by a group of visionaries: a woman and five clergymen who believed there must be a better way to meet the needs of local people. On October 16, 1887, this group created the Charity Organization Society, the first association set up to meet community needs by funding many charities while significantly reducing the number of appeals. It started the United Way model of using organized teams of workers to solicit employees in a variety of different businesses.

Today, United Way branches distribute more than $4 billion in philanthropic monies yearly to community agencies across the United States, to agencies like the Welfare Reform Liaison Project. Interestingly, the United Way, which started out primarily as a church-based effort by one woman, is not associated in the American psyche with religion. Rather, its focus is on the philanthropic efforts of the broader business community. Sure, many Catholic charities or a coalition of ministries are United Way members, but the religious roots of the United Way don't jump out at the average Joe. From watching mainly African-American professional athletes do their community service advertisements for the United Way over the years, one might get the impression that the United Way is a direct service provider, serving mainly blacks and minorities.

In a left-handed way, that is right, as many of the agencies that receive United Way distributions serve blacks and other minorities. In most cases, however, the only direct service the United Way delivers is its 211 referral system—a 911 of sorts—for emergency social service information. People in need can call 211 for help on a range of services and for referrals to the appropriate "helping organization."

But the irony is that, even with the good work being done, according to the National Black United Fund, an organization with twenty-two affiliates in cities around the United States, only 2 percent of the national philanthropic dollars go to black-led charities. Perhaps one reason for this is that many of those charities are beneath the local radar, housed in the black church, and have yet to built the sort of infrastructure to handle the kind of money that flowed, for example, into Odell's new organization. Although the Denver United Way made it clear that a woman and clergy were involved in its origination, its historical snapshot mentioned nothing of African Americans.

Perhaps the National Black United Fund, whose total dollar giving is dwarfed by the United Way of America's totals, started to help those smaller organizations emerging from the black church find an open hand for start-up funds when local United Way hands were tightfisted. That rationale was certainly one of the major justifications for the Bush administration's faith-based initiatives and focus on small black churches. As I have explained in greater detail in my previous work on the Bush faith-based initiative, had the initiative worked as hard in building the capacity of its target group—those small black churches that prayed with us at our "Moonie" meeting in Raleigh—as it did in changing laws, promoting their efforts in subtle political ways, I could have supported it. Had it not used highfalutin advertising on their target audiences, I almost could have been convinced that it was an honest effort at substantive change, much in line with the mission of the National Black United Fund. I do know that, in our community, churches that offer this or that kind of help, particularly the smaller black ministries, are not on the 211 system. I would guess that they aren't listed in many communities nationwide. And I would be willing to bet the store that university professors and black ministers are not lining up to work with each other the way Odell and I have.

Sadly, there are plenty of diamonds in the rough in communities all across our country, but a host of internal barriers in those nonprofits are just beneath the local radar. Moreover, roadblocks inside the ivory tower don't make it easy for professors to mine diamonds or polish the ones they do stumble on.

It is against the broader historical, very personal and local political context that one must view the *Your Way* newsletter article. Organizationally, there is no question that the United Way of Greensboro was proud to have received the Pinnacle Award from Gifts in Kind International. There is nothing like taking over first place from Sacramento—which at the time was the model of best practices for Gifts in Kind distribution—a community that had consciously been refining its Gifts in Kind program while the United Way of Greensboro, like most United Ways, didn't know how to refine theirs—that is, until the spirit of the Lord hit Odell in Elizabeth's Pizza.

There is little doubt in my mind or in Odell's that the same United Way that warned him that it didn't give money to churches just eighteen months earlier wanted to be in a partnership with a nonprofit affiliated with Mount Zion Baptist Church and Bishop George W. Brooks. Such a partnership could mirror the Weaver Foundation, help a black-led organization that helps black people, and do so with a bit more fanfare than Weaver could.

On the personal level, Neil Belenky, then president of United Way, had made a genuine commitment to do just that. Neil and I are friends who got to know each other while traveling to youth soccer games together; our sons were on the same high school and club teams. Neil was a Freedom Rider who had traveled to the South as a young man to participate in voter registration drives of the 1960s. Neil never advertised this information during his tenure as the local United Way leader.

Once Neil shared with Odell in a private meeting that he had been part of the voter registration drives in the 1960s, Odell asked him to conduct a workshop on his experiences at a faith summit, the Welfare Reform Liaison Project's biennial communitywide conference, outlined in the smoke-and-mirrors grant as a broad way to reduce system fragmentation (see appendix 3). Neil's personal efforts to get the most commitment to engage the United Way with black-led organizations, even those that were not part of the traditional United Way funding circle, was exemplary in my thirty years in the community. I am sure his commitment was rooted in his deep concern for social justice. Odell's trust and respect for Neil's community leadership went sky-high once Odell learned that the president of the United Way was in fact a Freedom Rider.

So it would not be fair to isolate one reason why the United Way of Greater Greensboro was a happy supporter of the Welfare Reform Liaison Project and a proud recipient of the 2000 Pinnacle Award from Gifts in Kind International. Nor would it be fair to say that Odell did not relish the partnership. In chapter 7, we showed a picture of Odell and Nathan Cook receiving the 1999 HUD award. But what we did not mention is that Odell asked HUD officials for two plaques, one for him and one for the United Way. Today, one can see both awards displayed prominently at both the United Way of Greater Greensboro and the Welfare Reform Liaison Project.

COMMUNITY CONNECTIONS ARE ESSENTIAL

What is most significant about the interlocking connection between the United Way of Greater Greensboro and the Welfare Reform Liaison Project is that Odell's successes became the United Ways successes, and the United Way was broadcasting the Welfare Reform Liaison Project's good works throughout both the community and the United Way's national network. A synergy was developing. It positioned the Welfare Reform Liaison Project for its leap into much greater community action and to make the final move to being from the church not of the church. It showed that the United Way was committed to the black community.

I don't want to wear out a much-quoted, cliché phrase from Tip O'Neill, speaker of the House of Representatives during the Reagan years, but all politics are indeed local. However, nothing captures the events that led to the Welfare Reform Liaison Project becoming a certified community leader than that cliché. Local social service politics in this case was not exactly the kind of politics one associates with backdoor dealing, handing out spoils to pass an unpopular social security tax, like the one Reagan and O'Neill brokered. Our local efforts were evolving against the backdrop of the racial politics of Greensboro. However, weaving in and out of the racial mine field in Greensboro and the Welfare Reform Liaison Project's corresponding successes cannot be divorced from the welfare reform policy of 1996 that kicked off our partnership, or from what unfolded in late 2001 and well into 2002. The patches on the quilt of community development have a good bit to do with Greensboro history, the national politics around Bush's faith-based initiative, my desire to have another permanent funding stream for the Welfare Reform Liaison Project, Odell's trust in me as both a professor and a friend, the United Way's presentation of itself to the community, Neil Belenky's personal efforts, and a healthy dose of Odell's charisma and his not knowing what he didn't know.

During 2000 and 2001, the Welfare Reform Liaison Project was enjoying its successes and building community partnerships. I was still badgering Odell that one- and two-year grants were not the answer to stable funding. He needed to make the distribution center the proverbial goose that laid golden eggs, or at least he needed to be on that goose's wings. He was moving as fast as circumstances allowed.

The nearly $500,000 yearly administrative fees that the distribution center produces today would have been ideal in 2000 and 2001 for the whole operation. But the business end of the center, while not exactly a moneymaker in those years, attracted the community from all parts. Still, by no means was it the large, refined income producer it is today.

By 2001, as the *Your Way* article noted, the United Way–Welfare Reform Liaison Project partnership was bringing in $14 million of corporate goods and redistributing them in large pallets to churches and nonprofits. It was earning money by charging an annual membership fee of $75 per nonprofit and church, and giving a one-time $120 voucher with initial membership. The United Way did not want anything to do with church membership, so Odell, whose organizational mission from day one was, in part, to help congregations expand their outreach to the needy, gladly assumed handling those membership dues and relationships.

Slowly, the retail outlet was growing to the point that a member organization, by using coupons bought from the Welfare Reform Liaison Project, could designate

people to shop for their personal needs. The United Way was keeping the administration fees for nonprofits, and Odell was responsible for churches. Ironically, it was
this early separation of responsibilities that gave the United Way and the Welfare
Reform Liaison Project what each wanted. Odell would build off the promise he made
in the smoke-and-mirrors grant to assess needs in the black churches and build an
organization that could respond in measurable ways. The United Way could help its
nonprofits and their clientele while taking credit for the whole partnership. It was a
win-win situation.

Still, even though the operation was beginning to bring in revenue, other grants
coming into the organization were subsidizing it, including more United Way smoke-
and-mirrors-like grants, but no finessing had to be done now. We did what we said
we would do and more. But supporting this and the other agency operations mainly
with grants was building an infrastructure on flimsy finances, and it worried me.

THE BISHOP'S ADVICE

Anyone who knows the grant game knows it is tricky. It is very complicated.
Different grants have different reporting requirements. Many are project specific and
don't allow for operating expenses beyond the specific project. To keep the operation funded and stable, not only does the bookkeeper become the most important
person in the agency at times; more times than anyone has dared to count, agencies
develop "new ventures" merely to keep current operations afloat in the guise of new
ventures. The old projects may indeed have been successful, but given the free-
market private funding game, the old widgets simply become less sexy to fund. That
combination requires squeaky clean bookkeeping and leadership in balancing innovation against having no real money to innovate.

This principle is necessary at times in an organization, but—in all seriousness—
how many more Odell Clevelands are out there who have God on their side but have
not found the capital and other resources to move beyond being average?

For a bookkeeper, leading a new venture like Odell's is like peering through the
lenses of a telescope, but in reverse. In a small town, with an even smaller philanthropic network, the last thing an organization wants to do is goof up, because the
incident won't be allowed to be isolated. News of failure, as we have shown with news
of success, spreads fast, furiously, and unfettered, often jeopardizing the organization's ability to stay on its feet and giving it little chance to retell the story to
provide balance. So excellent bookkeeping is very important, but it would be so
much better if it were balanced with some patience, community support, and good
old-fashioned chutzpah for taking some risks.

Because Odell was getting primarily one- and two-year grants from different
sources, there was always the struggle to get replacement money for the $30,000

from the original grant that was about to run out. He needed a long-term, stable funding base, at least until the distribution center could support a good portion of the operation. The United Way wanted the Welfare Reform Liaison Project to become a member on a three-year fast track, instead of the regular five years, which is the normal timeline for a new community agency to apply for membership and receive permanent funding.

I was against it. But it wasn't my advice Odell was following. It was that of Bishop George W. Brooks, cofounder of the Welfare Reform Liaison Project and Odell's pastor and friend who had been on the executive board of the United Way and knew its rules well. He didn't want Odell to make that fast-track move. And he told me that his reasoning was because he thought that United Way membership would eventually drown the Welfare Reform Liaison Project's affiliation with the spiritual aspects of Mount Zion, the church's very "reason for being."

The Welfare Reform Liaison Project, the largest diamond in the crown of Mount Zion's community efforts, would, in the bishop's thinking, no longer be either of the church or from it. Today, the agency is still very much from Mount Zion, despite how some insisted that it was of the church, particularly in the early days.

I simply thought Odell was too far outside of the box and would be corralled by the mainline United Way, and thus the project would never have the opportunity to be risky enough to fail or succeed. It was only when Odell and Fred Newman started to work together that the genius of the two leaders could be blended through debate, discussion, strategizing, planning, community engagement, and taking well-calculated risks—not with everything but with anything they planned out thoughtfully. The conserver Fred and the originator Odell made the Welfare Reform Liaison Project a very pragmatic organization. Odell didn't give up thousands of dollars in salary, a new company car, and stability for his family, or spend hours praying for guidance on his new path in life, just to be harnessed by a set of organizational rules from the United Way, rules that he didn't have a hand in shaping. Odell is not a rule breaker; he is a visionary, one who can look through the peephole in the tax rules that Gifts in Kind International adhered to and see truckloads of goods pouring into the Welfare Reform Liaison Project, a welfare program in Greensboro's business incubator complex. No one in the community could muster up that vision in their wildest dreams. (For a complete explanation of the tax codes that allowed Odell to redistribute goods, see appendix 4, which contains the article "In-Kind Contributions" by Ronald Fowler and Amy Henchey, which explains the complicated law in depth.)

From my perch as a cautious professor who was always engaged in the community but from the position of the university, I hypothesized that Odell was a bit too caught up in the jailhouse of his immediate successes, bred in part by the onslaught of money and accolades coming his way, without taking the necessary time to plan to pass the ultimate test of long-term nonprofit organizational stability—a permanent source of money, or a permanent enough one to be cautious and to develop plan A and plan B for crisis time, which the Welfare Reform Liaison Project now has done under the guidance and leadership of the board of directors, Fred Newman, Odell, and Kevin Odom, another key staff member.

CHAPTER 9

Church Gets Grant Lost by Jones

In this chapter, we circle back to some of the controversial racial concerns that sit just beneath the surface of nonprofit development by a black-led organization in Greensboro. As we noted previously, we circle back to this topic because it is surfaces in our community from time to time. For the record, all that we have said about Fred Newman's joining the agency actually came after what follows

A RAPID CHANGE

Things started to change fast, though, on November 27, 2001. The story of Earl Jones tells why.

Earl Jones, a prominent black political figure in Greensboro's political life, including being a city councilman at the time, ran the Community Action Agency (CAA), which serves Guilford County, of which Greensboro is the county seat. Starting in the spring of 2000, news stories started to appear increasingly about financial troubles at Jones's agency. The side of the racial divide from which one was watching Earl Jones often determined whether the sun was rising or setting on him, regardless of the slant or source of the news story.

No fewer than 604 *Greensboro News and Record* stories have mentioned something about Earl since the 1990s (for an example, see box on page 108). And in 2000, the stories increasingly focused on the financial troubles of his agency. The community action agency emerged as a key antipoverty program during President Johnson's War on Poverty of 1964. I was familiar with it firsthand, as I had worked in Montana with the local community action agency as a Vista volunteer in the early 1970s. Later, as a graduate student studying antipoverty policies, I followed the agency's political evolution and woes, and later its consolidation into the block grant system of moving federal programs to the states during the Reagan years. I watched from a distance after that. But I studied the local media's handling of Earl Jones's financial problems through the lens of a student of the community, of someone who knew Earl, someone who had a favorite student who worked at his agency, and through my personal connection to the program as a Vista volunteer.

By Nancy H. McLaughlin, *Greensboro News and Record*

The state agency that cut off money to City Councilman Earl Jones' nonprofit anti-poverty organization plans to meet Dec. 5 in Greensboro with local agencies interested in providing the same services. Lawrence Wilson, director of the state Office of Economic Opportunity, and his staff will meet at the old Guilford County Courthouse to answer questions about the federal Community Services Block Grant program, from which $800,000 is available for local agencies. The grant money is intended to help poor people find the jobs, education, housing or other means they need to become self-sufficient. The Guilford County Community Action Program got the grant until two years ago, when the state cut off all money to the agency, citing financial irregularities. The state is looking for a new agency to provide those services.

"A lot of people see money —but there are a lot of requirements," Wilson said. "We want everyone going into this to know what's before them." The state has contended that Jones, whose organization ran the program for nearly two decades, cannot account for the tax dollars his agency has received. In August, the U.S. Department of Health and Human Services ruled that North Carolina was within its rights to cut off Community Action's money. Jones maintains the state acted illegally and failed to give Community Action a chance to correct problems. Both he and a group of clients plan lawsuits, he says.

Because of new federal guidelines, local agencies already providing services to low-income people within Guilford County will get a preference over agencies already recognized by the Office of Economic Opportunity in surrounding counties. Applicants will be rated on a number of factors, including what they are chartered to do and what others who have funded them in the past have to say about their programs. Already, organizations ranging from the Salvation Army of Greensboro to the Pulpit Forum and Caring Services of High Point have contacted Wilson about the process.

"We have an infrastructure already in place so we could quickly get the services to the people who need them the most," said Capt. Ward Matthews of the Salvation Army, where the poor already can get emergency assistance, counseling for addictions, job training and help learning how to balance their checkbooks. At the Open Door Ministries of High Point, the money would also be used to reach more people than those already being served. "The demand is definitely there," said Stephen Key, Open Door's director. Wilson, whose office administers the grant, says he hopes to have a recommendation for the state secretary of health and human services, who will then make a recommendation to the governor, by March. Applications will be available at the December meeting.

I really had no judgment as to whether there had been any wrongdoing. When I saw that the state of North Carolina had taken Jones's block grant program away and freed the funds for local competition, it was simply game on for Odell and me. I kept telling Odell that this was a different kind of federal grant, one that came through the state directly to agencies. It was like Head Start money—it might get cut or increased on the basis of the political winds, but it was not likely to vanish altogether. The continuation of this type of federal legislation that funds community action agencies was in America's political fibers. It was part of the federal system of block grants to the states, and the state office acted as overseer, which administers or oversees the federal program as block grants move federal funds from legislation to the states. This was part of Ronald Reagan's new federalism—originally 167 separate federally administered programs were put into twelve block grants and shifted to the states.

Odell was clueless about community action agencies. I gave him something to read, but the content never really penetrated. Just like I could not envision truckloads of goods, new warehouses, and new revenue streams, plus putting people in simulated work training, he could not see what I saw. I saw the agencies in this community, very capable agencies at that—like Salvation Army, Goodwill Industries, and Guilford Child Development—competing with us for this grant. Yet as capable as they were, I deeply believed we could win this funding and get the necessary support from key players to write support letters, as the Welfare Reform Liaison Project was making the kind of positive splash that we have noted so far. I had been a grant judge on numerous occasions, so I approach grant writing as if I were still a grant judge. I saw similar narratives from agencies with similar boilerplates of material to include in a grant application slowly lulling the panel of judges, with ten to fifteen applications, into a stupor. We had no boilerplate yet, especially for this kind of grant. So I knew that if we could jolt the judges with brand-spanking-new ideas about how the Welfare Reform Liaison Project would get hard-to-place people in the workforce, and if we could demonstrate that, though young, the agency had a proven record for keeping people in the workforce, and if we could lace the proposal with positive energetic words throughout, then we would have a chance to shake six or seven judges into reading and scoring our proposal wide eyed.

On January 20, 2001, President Bush launched his faith-based initiative. As a backdrop, the political and social atmosphere, still stunned from the events of 9/11, was amenable, perhaps more so than at any time in recent memory, to accept the idea of a faith-based nonprofit competing for federal community action agency status. In such a political environment, at least the Welfare Reform Liaison Project would not be tossed out because it was faith-based. Even the letterhead that went to the review committee had at the very bottom in fine but clear print a quote from Matthew 25:35–36. "In His Service" was gone but not forgotten.

Although the evaluation criteria made it clear that applicants had to be a 501(c)(3) nonprofit organization separate from the church, the Welfare Reform Liaison Project's connections to a highly regarded black church in Greensboro would help, and not hurt, the chances of winning, more so than had been the case in other periods. Odell and the staff prayed together before the completed application left the agency. I never prayed for this one. I had Odell over to the "man cave" office every day for a week. We worked several hours a day, crafting each section into a proposal, so that when I switched hats to be a tired grant judge, I would award every single one of the 110 points on the tally sheet (see figure 12; for the complete rating criteria, see appendix 5). The grant nailed every criterion!

Applying Agency	Section I				Section II			Section III				Bonus Points	TOTAL Points
	Sub-Sect. 1	Sub-Sect. 2	Sub-Sect. 3	Sub-Sect. 4	Sub-Sect. 1	Sub-Sect. 2	Sub-Sect. 3	Sub-Sect. 1	Sub-Sect. 2	Sub-Sect. 3	Sub-Sect. 4		
Maximum Points →	5	10	25	15	10	10	5	5	5	5	5	10	110

Ranking
From the highest scorer to the lowest, list the Applicants below.

Rank	Name of Applicant	Rank	Name of Applicant
#1		#6	
#2		#7	
#3		#8	
#4		#9	
#5		#10	

FIGURE 12. *Tally Sheet*

Of course, Odell would say, and still says, that all of this was the hand of God. Enough evidence was mounting that he may have been on to something. I started to feel that the moon was in the seventh house and Jupiter was aligned with Mars. As an Aquarian, I really felt that this was the dawning of the age of the Welfare Reform Liaison Project, with a stable funding base on the horizon.

I also knew that if Odell won this funding, it would be the last time I would have to write a grant proposal for the Welfare Reform Liaison Project, as there would be enough funds to hire a person who could work on grants alongside a far more advanced Odell Cleveland. Odell was learning about grant writing from the inside. He would soon be able to collaborate with a grant writer on an equal footing, and without my advice. I really wanted to give my blessing to him and release him from my mentoring throngs—and to be satisfied that he knew this game from the insider's view.

During much of this journey, I truly have been a student as much as a mentor to Odell. But on this occasion, I needed to teach hard and fast. I prepared Odell to go toe to toe with his eventual grant writer—Fred Newman, who like me teaches grant writing. Fred and I have sat on grant-judging panels together, and he was also a Vista volunteer who knew community action agencies firsthand. Not knowing at that time who would replace me, I wanted Odell at my side the entire time for that reason, and I wanted to teach him what I thought a community action agency for the twenty-first century looked like on paper.

In the smoke-and-mirrors grant and before that in the little blue book with his business plan he carried around and distributed to community people, Odell had a plan, the framework for the next stage of development. This community action grant was the plan. If he won that grant, he not only would again face local scrutiny but also would become part of a national network of more than one thousand community action agencies, some of which have existed since the 1960s. He also would be a new and different kid on the block, one from the church but not of it (for the text of the grant proposal, see appendix 6). But the grant would pave the way for Fred Newman and other staff members to change the internal systems of the organization and balance them with the external mission.

THE PROFESSOR RETURNS

As Odell tells it, I would be sitting at my computer, with him at my right side. I would ask him what he thought each criterion meant. He says that I stared intently in space while thinking of what to write, looking like the nerdy professor, which at times I am. But I was actually thinking of just the right translation of his words, ones that only a preacher like Odell could come up with, and the kinds that could make Rodin's Thinker use two fists to ponder. I needed words, though, that the judges not only understood but also felt.

We went through this for every criterion. Then we worked like artists to construct an appendix that would get us extra credit on this test, an exam that tested both us. Odell insisted on sending along a film about the agency with the proposal package.

"No one does that," I told him. He blew me off and sent it anyway. Scuttlebutt has it that the film was a key piece for the appendix of the grant application.

Years later, as we talked about the CAA grant for this book, Odell turned to me and said: "Wine, you were the professor when you needed to be. There was no syllabus; there were no other students. I was not a traditional learner. I was from the community and you were from the university, teaching me in a way that I could learn about something I needed to learn! That is what has to happen when you professors come out of the ivory tower into the community. You professors are smart! You just need to get out more." He was right, we do.

GETTING THE GRANT

On February 13, 2002, fewer than five years after our first United Way grant, the Welfare Reform Liaison Project Inc. was named the "eligible entity to provide Community Services Block Grant Program services" in an official letter from the then governor of North Carolina, Mike Easley. It was official: the Welfare Reform Liaison Project would now receive stable funding to be of the community. Or at least that is what we thought.

On February 14, the *Greensboro News and Record* ran an article on the grant with the headline "Church Gets Grant Lost by Jones; The Welfare Reform Liaison Project Is an Outreach of Mount Zion Baptist Church on Alamance Church Road."

The grant proposal left the project on January 17, 2002, shrouded in the staff's prayer, and I began calling Odell daily throughout February to see whether he had received any word on the status of the grant. I was getting nervous. On February 13, I called Odell. He quietly, almost whispering, told me that he had gotten word forty-five minutes earlier that the Welfare Reform Liaison Project received the grant and that I was to be at a meeting at two o'clock with the executive staff of Mary Reaves, Earlene Thomas, Odell, and Nancy McLean, to discuss how they were going to talk to the press about the grant at a four-o'clock press meeting.

Odell was confident and low key, but I exploded with joy over the phone the same way I did when we hit on that first grant. Deep down, my feelings were hurt that he hadn't called me earlier. I thought perhaps that it was because I hit the "winning basket" while he was on the bench in the "man cave." In reality, he was stunned and happy, and he didn't get around to calling, so my speculation was just a part of the narrative—spoken and unspoken—we have had and still have with each other. But I knew he would get his playing time, and plenty of it for the next eight years and beyond. I arrived at the distribution center on Lee Street to see the group sitting quietly, very confidently but not smugly and relieved yet somewhat in disbelief. We began to get happy and started laughing, but the seriousness of being "of" the community and of having a solid base of funding to go along with the distribution efforts was sinking in.

We all agreed that, in talking to Nancy McLaughlin, the reporter for the

Greensboro News and Record, Odell would emphasize that the Welfare Reform Liaison Project was going to work for the betterment of the community. The headlines the next day had a clear message, however: the black-led Mount Zion church—not the Welfare Reform Liaison Project, the separate 501(c)(3)—was going to do right with the money. That was something that the black councilman Earl Jones—in some quarters, a controversial community figure—was allegedly unable to do; namely, spend tax dollars prudently and legitimately. It became clear that the Welfare Reform Liaison Project would have to show results before it was considered the premier workforce development agency, and that would be until powers bigger than the agency would set it free.

BEING OF THE CHURCH NATIONALLY

Ironically, less than a year after the "Church Gets Grant" headline in Greensboro, the Welfare Reform Liaison Project and Odell would be chastised for being a faith-based organization at the National Community Action Management Academy: Being of Service training conference. To attend the training, the agency had to submit an application and be accepted. There were about fifty other attendees representing seven other community action agencies in North Carolina. The leader of the national community action movement, David Bradley, a highly regarded advocate and spokesperson for community action nationally, was giving a State of the Union type address on the history of and threats to community action agencies. As Bradley enumerated the threats, he shocked both Odell and Odell's staff by saying that George Bush's faith-based initiative was the biggest threat to community action agencies because the Bush administration wanted to shift community action dollars to faith-based organizations.

Odell stewed for a while as Bradley ranted against faith-based organizations. Odell slowly slipped his hand into the increasingly tense air that forty-four other people were breathing, people who knew, as did Bradley, that the Welfare Reform Liaison Project was faith-based. Odell patiently waited for Bradley to acknowledge him, and when that happened, the room became even tenser.

"You were never supposed be here, and you were never supposed to be able to compete for community action dollars," Bradley said to Odell before Odell had a chance to say anything. To Odell's surprise and deep pain, the mainly black audience started applauding. Odell remained standing, and when the applause died down, he looked David Bradley straight in the eye, much like the undersized basketball star had done in his college days when he took on six foot ten inch centers, and said: "But we are here. We are a part of the community action family. Now what are you going to do?" Odell, a reverend from the black church, then turned and looked into the faces of the 80 percent black representatives from other community action agen-

cies. In his stern preacher voice, he queried each one of them rhetorically and loudly, the way a preacher speaks to the congregation and to the individual simultaneously: "You are not going to clap for me now?"

Odell purposely said those words with a tone loaded in coded rings. He coupled
those rings with a puzzled look of sad betrayal in his eyes. His message to his mainly black churchgoing brethren was this: "You clapped for the white guy and you
won't clap for me? I am your family!"

"Wine, remember how you felt when you were at that meeting in Raleigh?" Odell
asked me years later. "Bradley blindsided me."

The moderator had stepped in and cut the tension by calling for a break. Despite
all the preparation we had done in Greensboro to be from the church, of the community, and not of the church, once Odell and the Welfare Reform Liaison Project stepped
into the national community action game, others were again defining him and the
project. And he wasn't prepared. This reversal in definitions was shocking to him. Yet
as he recalls: "I had five staff members next to me there who were excited to be in
the community action family, and we were painted as illegitimate. What kind of leader
would I be if I didn't stand up for all we had done to get into this new family?"

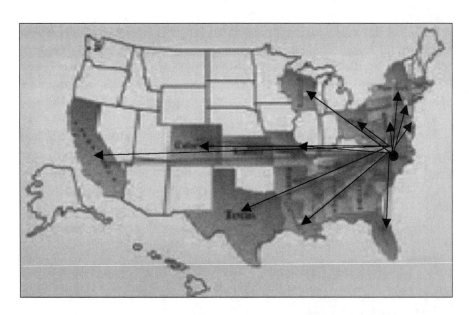

FIGURE 13. *Map of Places the Welfare Reform Liaison Project Has Consulted*

PERFORMANCE

Performance is what has legitimized the Welfare Reform Liaison Project in every venue. Performance came from Odell's leadership, not from words or headlines. As a map of the Welfare Reform Liaison Project's national influence demonstrates (figure 13), the undersized and overmatched Odell Cleveland was going to outwork all 999 other community action agencies to become the model of a twenty-first-century poverty-reducing agency. Humiliation transferred to an already-deep motivation to be the best.

To be fair to Bradley, he has been more favorable now to faith-based partnerships with community action agencies, but to date, the only declared faith-based nonprofit in the nation's community action family is Guilford County's Community Service block grant designee, the Welfare Reform Liaison Project.

CHAPTER 10

The Road Back from Jerusalem

In our first grant, we said that, as a result of the original research project, we
would hold a community meeting, which Odell later called the Faith Summit.
In this chapter, we show continuity amid change. Every two years since the inception
of the Welfare Reform Liaison Project, the project has held a community meeting.
This chapter shows how all the agency's work came together, and it illustrates how
the project is of the community and from the church.

THE FAITH SUMMIT: BUILDING COMMUNITY

In late fall of 2008, an interfaith group of clergy from Greensboro traveled together
to Israel. Nearly two dozen local religious leaders toured the country and took in the
Holy Land's many important sites.

The bonds Greensboro's clergy developed with one another on that trip held
after they returned from Jerusalem, which further widened and strengthened the
community's many interlocking partnerships.

Those ties were on full display at the Guilford County Faith Summit in 2009, the
Welfare Reform Liaison Project's sixth since the inaugural summit in 1999. One of the
sessions at the summit was dedicated to the interfaith clergy trip to Israel, and the
session began with an eighteen-minute-long multimedia presentation of their time
in the Holy Land. The Copycents division of the Welfare Reform Liaison Project inci-
dentally produced the video.

Reverend Richard Johnson, the spiritual leader of We Are One Christian
Fellowship in Greensboro and the son of a Mississippi sharecropper, recounted his
emotional sojourn at Yad Vashem, Israel's official Holocaust museum. His voice
cracked as he recounted seeing pictures of children behind barbed-wire fencing
awaiting their eventual slaughter.

Reverend Adrian Starks, another African-American minister and leader of
Anderson Grove Baptist Church in Greensboro, told of a moving experience while
praying at the Wailing Wall in Jerusalem. Before leaving Greensboro, the ministers
had been encouraged to bring with them notes from their congregants to place in
the wall. As the holiest place in Judaism, the Wailing Wall is considered the closest

physical place to God, and the faithful put notes between its giant stones in the belief that God will hear believers' entreaties.

Reverend Starks placed notes of prayer from his parishioners in the wall's many cracks, but one note fell to the ground. A young ultra-Orthodox Jewish boy next to him picked the note up and handed it to Reverend Starks so he could take the final step in his 6,200-mile special delivery. Reverend Starks connected that young boy's wordless deed with those of the young Jesus, who two thousand years earlier had surely walked on the same ground.

Just as important, the interfaith trip allowed for the clergy to bond in other, more earthly ways. The Copycents video featured a clip of Reverend Terry Moore Painter, the chaplain at our large community hospital, kicking back in the Dead Sea. She's got a tough job, one I doubt I could handle for even a day, so she deserved the break. I'm sure the others did, too, and those moments of relaxing together helped cement bonds even more.

At the Guilford County Faith Summit in 2009, a panel of religious leaders from Greensboro's major white and black congregations spoke and answered questions for nearly an hour after the screening of the Holy Land video (see appendix 7).

As I heard the words of Reverend Diane Givens Moffett, leader of St. James Presbyterian Church, I thought back to how the seeds Odell and I had planted more than a decade earlier were blooming. Reverend Moffett framed the relational aspect of the trip as the seeds for a better Greensboro community.

Doubtlessly, the video was causing flashbacks in my head the way it was for the trip's participants, including Odell, who was sitting in the front of the room in his ever-present business suit moderating the event. I then heard Reverend Sid Batts of the First Presbyterian Church, Mo Seller's church, which had given the Welfare Reform Liaison Project $25,000 a decade earlier. Sid stated that the trip had enabled him, in time of need, to call any of the twenty-three clergy for help without hesitation. He named Odell specifically.

I hadn't boarded a plane for Israel, but in more ways than one, I was on that trip, too. I knew many of the clergy more than casually and had been to most of the places they visited in Israel. I was filled with joy that Odell and his wife, Beverly, went to the birthplace of Jesus, knowing what that meant for them spiritually.

My rabbi, Fred Guttman, led the trip. I had been on a trip he led before, and I knew how much the group learned from his incredible teaching. Months earlier, Fred had called me to ask whether I thought Odell would be interested in going on the trip. A decade earlier, I might have had to explain to Odell the importance of such networking. By 2009, however, Odell was the master of such matters. I gave Odell's number to Fred and suggested he give him a call.

Over the years, I have worked on important community concerns with several of the Christian clergy who went on the trip. I've also worked on more personal concerns with them. When I saw the full screen shot of Reverend Frank Dew of Greensboro Urban Ministry in his baseball cap and T-shirt, I was back marveling at his three-year-old daughter Christy's flowing long hair. Our daughters had gone to the College Hill Coop Child Care Center together at Presbyterian Church of the Covenant twenty-one years earlier.

The Copycents production was quite a sight. The still shots and the video showed partnerships in action to all those assembled at the faith summit. Black and white, Christian and Jewish, large and small congregations—all those clerical sisters and brothers with ministries in the Greensboro community square were united in the Holy Land. Twenty-three religious leaders who touch thousands in our community, some of whom never met each other, were arm-in-arm in their common spiritual cradle, united yet different, undoubtedly integrated.

The seeds in that little blue book and the smoke-and-mirrors grant that we had planted years earlier germinated and budded in the Holy Land in ways we had only hoped for in our dreams. As Rabbi Guttman wrote in the *Greensboro News and Record* after they came back from Israel:

> In recent times, religious communities in Greensboro have become "siloed" from one another along denominational and racial lines. But that wasn't the case for us. The clergy on the trip represented a minimum of nine different denominations. Eight were African American. We hope that better interfaith relationships among clergy will lead to mutual cooperation on community projects that will benefit the people of Greensboro.
>
> As one of our participants said, "I had to come 6,200 miles to Israel to really get to know the minister who pastors the church across the street from me."

To paraphrase Dr. Martin Luther King's quote: It has been said more than once, correctly or not, that Greensboro is most segregated at eleven o'clock on Sunday mornings. Not so in the Holy Land, or at the 2009 faith summit.

Because of that trip, Greensboro would become less segregated, less tense racially, and less tense between faiths than it was in 2001. That year, the first "social capital" report commissioned by the foundation leadership of Greensboro and overseen by the Community Foundation of Greater Greensboro announced: "Overall, the study shows that citizens in Guilford County attend places of worship more, volunteer their time and talents more, and give more money to charities when compared

From: Fred Guttman
Sent: Monday, February 22, 2010
To: Odell Cleveland
Subject: Reminder—Community Interfaith meeting with Senator Kay Hagan
RSVP Needed

Reminder—*Community Interfaith meeting with Senator Kay Hagan*

RSVP Numbers Needed

7:30 PM

March 7, 2010
Temple Emanuel
1129 Jefferson Rd
Bring 15 people plus clergy from your congregation, preferably leadership or
people who are active in community.

7:30-8 PM – Dessert and fellowship
8 PM – Program to include
Opening prayer
Report on homelessness in Greensboro and how congregations can become
involved. Senator Hagan is introduced and speaks on her perception as to what
is happening in Congress, especially the Senate.

Q & A
Closing prayer

IMPORTANT NOTE—We would like to have an estimate of how many people are
coming from the church by next Monday, March 1. Please send me an email on
this. (Dessert will be served)

Looking forward to our being together.

to national averages. However, the area ranks below national averages when it comes
to trusting one another, socializing with friends and playing an active role in the
political process."

The trip to Israel in 2008 built off of the strengths the study found in the
religious community in Greensboro by hammering away very creatively at some of
the barriers that led to mistrust. Until 2007, deep trust was still lacking in
Greensboro, as noted in a follow-up "social capital" study in 2006 supported by
Greensboro's philanthropic community and overseen by the Community Foundation
of Greater Greensboro.

During President Bush's faith-based initiative, I had little patience for the left or the right. Little attention was spent organizing the collective group into a community-minded interest group that could learn from and teach political leaders about common concerns that make communities healthier. The trip to Israel did just that, as an e-mail and invitation to the other trip members from Rabbi Fred Guttman demonstrates (see page 120).

The faith community town hall, orchestrated by Rabbi Guttman, was a full house and full of education about homelessness and tough questions from the left and right, and equally hard-hitting responses from U.S. Senator Kay Hagan. It reminded me of a mini faith summit.

Two of the objectives of the little blue book—that quasi business plan that Odell handed out to every community leader imaginable in 1997 and 1998, when the Welfare Reform Liaison Project was moving from Mount Zion's emergency assistance operation to being a community-based nonprofit—were to "hold a conference of fifty churches" and "network with groups of similar interest." In our first grant, in 1998, the fifth project activity listed was "to hold a community conference of [Welfare] Work First Recipients, religious leaders, community agencies and [Department of Social Service] workers to address the problems of poor women." We went on to say, "[T]he conference will be to talk about what the social service community is lacking, what the church community has, and what both systems need to do to effectively address the problems that are going to be faced by women and children."

MEETING WITH THE U.S. SENATOR

When it all boils down, the goals we had back in 1998 are along the same lines as those Rabbi Guttman was trying to accomplish a dozen years later with the post-Israel meeting with Senator Hagan. We were all trying to use the strengths of the religious community to shore up the mistrust in the community at large, the mistrust starkly pointed out by the 2001 "social capital" report.

The room was packed at the meeting with Hagan, filled with community leaders who collectively represented roughly thirty thousand people. Our senator, who was also a member of the First Presbyterian Church, was indeed in an interesting position that night.

Mainline white and black congregations have been quietly and unceremoniously partnering in community efforts since the Reagan cuts in social services, and they have done some gut-wrenching work with and on behalf of the poor. But their efforts rarely had an audience, with all the attention of major political leaders going to right-wing religious groups and their like. That night in Greensboro, they had an audience with some big backing. They traded thoughts with someone who could maybe, just maybe, strengthen already-existing local partnerships. A new seed was planted.

If Bishop George W. Brooks had his way, the Welfare Reform Liaison Project would hold a faith summit every year at Mount Zion, instead of every other year. But the time it takes to orchestrate such an event is too much to do annually. The number of those attending the event has grown from one hundred to five hundred, and the likes of Jim Wallis, Jeremy White, of the White House Office of Faith-Based and Community Initiatives, staff from our senator's office, and numerous state and local politicians came to the summit to mix with social service providers, religious leaders, and recipients of the Welfare Reform Liaison Project's program services. At the 2009 summit, the big name to join us was Melissa Rogers, an appointee to President Obama's Faith Commission.

The focus of the summits changed over the years, of course. At the first one in 1999, talk centered on what Greensboro's institutions could do to tackle welfare to work. In 2009, discussion revolved around what a lagging economy meant for the faith and social services communities, and for the human beings whose lives were being torn up by economic calamity.

But throughout the years, the spirit was always the same—putting common unity back into *community*.

During the 2009 faith summit, I got a big hug from Sinda, one of the first program graduates whom Odell had lured back to the project from a job in the community. She told me I was the first Jew she had ever met, and that she wanted to know more about my people. It might've taken a 6,200-mile intercontinental trip and six faith summits to get to that point, but if there were any doubts left in my mind about the possibilities for finding common ground, that hug erased them on the spot.

When you get right down to it, Sinda made it clear that day, we aren't that much different after all.

Conclusion

Quite often we sanitize the pain people experience by describing it with nameless and faceless concepts—the homeless, the hungry, the disabled, the old, the sick, the poor, the laid off. But for Odell, and for me as well, those concepts have very real faces to them, and they look at us every day in Greensboro.

We see people struggling beyond human imagination to overcome some of the most painful and gut-gnarling concerns. They are every bit as human as the rest of us, which ought to make their pain gut-gnarling for those lucky enough not to suffer their fate.

As George Orwell wrote in his 1961 work *Down and Out in Paris and London:* "The mass of the rich and the poor are differentiated by their incomes and nothing else, and the average millionaire is only the average dishwasher dressed in a new suit. Change places, and handy dandy, which is the justice, which is the thief? Everyone who has mixed on equal terms with the poor knows this quite well."

Or as Odell would put it, the Welfare Reform Liaison Project's contract with Men's Wearhouse was not to provide poor men with a new suit but to provide men with unfortunate pasts a renewed spirit to compete on equal terms from the inside. If this is how Odell's faith works, then so be it. Praise the Lord!

From the day Odell and I first talked in the locker room after our "geezer game," Odell and the Welfare Reform Liaison Project have worked to put new suits on people's spirits. The means to get there have varied over the years, but the mission has stayed the same. Poor people have changed their approach to life and have made some financial strides in the process, earning more than $7 million dollars in wages collectively and participating as taxpayers—instead of "draining the system."

And the community is changing in its willingness to follow in Odell's tailwinds. A little while back I was at the Welfare Reform Liaison Project's offices in the video production wing, as I have often been during the past thirteen years. I started talking to Thomas, a man who has been through hell and back. I was near tears, not so much from the painfulness of Thomas's story—which was more than enough to make a grown man cry—but because I could see how Odell's program had worked for Thomas, as it has for many others. Odell's spirit was alive in all the people, organizations, and communities he had influenced.

I was thankful to have been a utility player in it all. Talking to Thomas, I realized that Odell was right when he told me to get out into the community more. Odell's fight and his can-do attitude were literally pulling that beaten-down man's spirit out of him. Thomas, a fiftysomething white guy who had been hit by a combination of tangled economics and personal tragedy, was walking around the Welfare Reform Liaison Project talking about playing life to win.

Men and women like Thomas were being trained to make DVDs, like the compelling one on the interfaith clergy trip to Israel. They were on the job, learning media production skills, and the value of the program for them was impossible to calculate.

That day, Thomas was studiously pondering ways to turn an hour of footage into an eight-minute clip. The footage captured a day in the life of Robert, one of those guys everyone has seen on a busy intersection in a big city, holding up a sign that reads "Will Work for Food." Robert follows his wife from nursing home to nursing home, visiting her daily. Neither the clip nor Thomas elaborated why she was in a nursing home and had to move every so often.

Thomas and the team of media production students he leads were searching for a way they could edit the video for competition in the Faces of Poverty, a contest the Welfare Reform Liaison Project runs. Prizes of $1,000, $800, and $600 go to the three best productions in the eight-team student competition. Thomas's niece gave a couple of bucks regularly to Robert, so she asked him whether he would mind being interviewed. Thomas did the film shoot and edits with his team, but his niece conducted the interview.

Thomas said to me three times that day that if it weren't for his sister, her disability check, which covered rent and food stamps, he could be right where Robert was, on the street by day and living in a makeshift home in the woods at night. Both men were willing as hell to do any kind of work, as Robert's sign said.

If George Orwell was right—and in Robert's case, he right was on the money— then most of those men and women you see holding up "Will Work for Food" signs are not even making enough to find a room every couple of days to clean themselves, let alone driving the Cadillacs all welfare moms supposedly cruised around in.

At one point, Odell turned to Thomas and told him that I was his mentor. It was a bit ironic, I thought. There I was, the university big shot who supposedly mentored the big boss, and it was actually I who was being mentored, by Thomas, Robert, and Odell. They were teaching me what this whole adventure was really about.

Odell asked Thomas how he felt being a white guy at Welfare Reform Liaison Project, "with all these black people around." Thomas looked at him puzzled.

"I never thought about it," he said. In that man's soul—where it really counted—the Welfare Reform Liaison Project was the color of water. It was a place of all faiths and of no faiths.

Each step of the agency's development was possible because of the previous one. That the Welfare Reform Liaison Project is what it is today is in large part because, at each step along the way, Odell's agenda became further intertwined with that of the broader community.

In 1997, Odell was struggling to graduate from a part-time theology program at Hood Theological Seminary. Today, he teaches a section on community practice at the University of North Carolina at Greensboro.

Also in 1997, the Bryan Venture Grant Fund of the United Way awarded the Welfare Reform Liaison Project its first grant, for $25,000. Today, Odell sits on the United Way's board of directors and on its finance committee.

And as these words—this book's last—were being written, we learned that Odell had just been named to the Bryan Venture Grant Fund's selection committee, the same one that awarded Odell that first $25,000 in 1997 and the same one I had served on years earlier. There could no longer be any doubt, if any still existed: Odell Cleveland had undeniably become of the community, serving "In His Service" those who need it most.

Postscript

This story is about Odell Cleveland and the journey Odell and I took together over the past dozen or so years. But there have been many others on the Welfare Reform Liaison Project's bus, and here they deserve a word or two of mention: as a pracademic, they made my life fun and easy during my many hours at the Welfare Reform Liaison Project.

There's Mary, Nancy, and Earlene, the women whose spiritual juices still flavor the Welfare Reform Liaison Project even though case management is now contracted out. Tonji, Vanessa, and Christi worked hard to keep the students I placed at the project busy and on task. Vanessa and Christi were once students in my class where I placed interns.

There is Deborah Moore. When Deborah was a Department of Social Services manager, she was part of that original contracting process. Today she is Welfare Reform Liaison Project's director of training and brings the agency a world of experience. Today, like Fred Newman, she's an important passenger on Odell's bus and provides valuable leadership and insight into how the Department of Social Services, an important partner, operates.

Marwan, or "Mo," the chief executive officer of cleanup and logistics, has been at the Welfare Reform Liaison Project almost since day one. If given a minute of ear time, he will tell anyone who is willing to listen how Odell turned his unbelievably shaky life around. Mo always stops to give me his regular warm hug.

There was Harrell, always zipping by in his wheelchair and waving. And Benita, with her incredible smile and goodwill, rushing to hug me in front of everyone, always making me feel honored. Sinda and Linda add to the vibrant spirit of the distribution center. Ron Brooks is an active board member but came through the ranks of the Welfare Reform Liaison Project's program. When I told my daughter Hannah about Ron being selected to the board of directors, she said, "Daddy he was a thug!" Hannah spent time at the distribution center for four summers during high school and college and knew the "old" Ron. Ron bought a home, had a child, and found and kept a full-time job since Hannah's time at the project. And there have been great board leaders, some of whom I got to know, like Ron Surgeon. He always took time to mentor my students. Lee McAllister and Ron Surgeon among others played a crucial role in making the transition from a ministry to a top-tier nonprofit.

And of course there's Sandy Woodard, the real boss of the Welfare Reform Liaison Project. No one gets past her gaze upon entering the agency's offices.

Jerome and Kevin simply make me happy to be alive. They are such wonderful people whom I passed regularly en route to the DVD production outfit. Jeff Black is the genius of the unit; he turned what Odell called my "boring research" into an interesting fifteen-minute DVD that I've already presented at three conferences. Terres and Ish were always there to lend a helping hand.

And last but never least, although we discussed Fred Newman's joining the Welfare Reform Liaison Project at length in an earlier chapter, he deserves another mention here. He is *the* Fred Newman, and that's as high a compliment as can be made.

EPILOGUE

For the Students Who Read this Book

We passed over some points that students might want to consider in thinking about organizational development in a community context:

- We talked about the working philosophy of most welfare agencies at the time welfare reform came along. Large bureaucracies don't change quickly. Think about what it might take to make a large or small change in your welfare, public health, or mental health system.

- We talked about the reality of implementation of a national policy locally and how reality bumps into the theory. What are examples from your experiences of how realities on the ground differ from the intended ideas of a policy or program initiative? How might the disconnect that occurs between policy theories and implementation realities be remedied?

- In many parts of the book, we alluded to but did not go into much detail about the need for careful planning steps and research before launching programs. Can you think of instances in which good data or careful planning could have prevented problems with programs with which you are familiar?

- We made very strong points about the reluctance of social service funders to fund applied research that supports program development. Can you think of ways to educate local funders about the value of research? Can you think of ways researchers can make their work more valuable to funders? Do you have concrete examples of the successful use of research?

- We talked about the tightrope that Reverend Cleveland had to walk in getting community support for his program and made an extra effort to point out how he needed to use different ways to speak to different audiences and use the spirit in which he presented himself. He went through a learning curve. What are several different ways that you might present your favorite agency or organizations to a ten-year-old, a banker, a foreign student in the United States for the first time, and an elderly person who is a different race from your own?

- We made a point of discussing the realities of the local money game. Why do you think we often said we play the money game to win? Should people have to compete to "win for the poor"?

- In various parts of the book, we speak of different styles of leadership in nonprofits at different stages of development. What are some ways leaders might grow with changes in the community and organizational environments?

- We spent quite a bit of time before, during, and after writing this book discussing and arguing over the question of being of the church and from the church. How do you think we handled this in the book? Do you know of organizations that are in circumstances similar to ours in the early years of moving into the community? How do they handle this delicate matter?

- We noted the multiple hurdles most welfare-to-work clients face. What are some organizational, community, educational, and media strategies to change some of these barriers at the policy level, at the community level, and at the practice level?

- We emphasize the need to diversify funding sources and to be entrepreneurial. How can nonprofits make money through activities that haven't been thought of yet or haven't been employed in your community? How might such new ways be tested? What would the story line be?

- We glossed over how we were almost blindsided by a contract that shifted costs from the welfare agency to our nonprofit. Do you know of examples of this kind of cost shifting, and how it can be stopped, avoided, or modified? Is it natural for cash-strapped government organizations to shift costs to smaller nonprofits? Are there assumptions in the process that have not been tested in practice or through research?

- Given the existing competition for scarce funds and the need to build community partnerships, how can competition and cooperation exist side by side, and compete for the same scarce dollars, when two organizational and community activities are seemingly at odds?

- We showed you how the grants game and reporting requirements create the need for excellent and adaptive bookkeeping. How does a leader go about integrating and balancing the perspectives of the chief financial officer and the board around financial accountability, with the need for practitioners to have enough resources to succeed in solving, managing, or preventing important community problems?

- What did you think about the faith summit? We found that community providers, politicians, academics, and recipients of service enjoy sharing information and collaborating in new ways if you just bring them together. Can communities hold regular gatherings without the faith community? Are churches community organizations? Can they be community organizations if they are exclusive?

- We spent many hours writing and arguing about race, knowing that the people in our own community would read this story. We will have gotten it right for some and wrong for others. What do you think about how we handled racial concerns in this book? Do you think that our ability to transcend race between us individually was luck, God's hand at work, or two stubborn old athletes not wanting to lose at something we thought we could win at—helping the poor a bit better than had we not tried at all?

We think there might be questions that we could have asked or you might want to ask us, and we are both believers that the only bad question is the one not asked. So if you have a question, feel free to contact either of us: Odell Cleveland at revcleve99@triad.rr.com and Bob Wineburg at bobwineburg@gmail.com.

Please visit us on Facebook: Odell Cleveland, Bob Wineburg.

APPENDIX 1

American Recovery and Reinvestment Act: Stimulus Money for Rapid Job Training

We would be remiss if we didn't note that the Welfare Relief Liaison Program (WRLP) was chosen to receive $1.2 million in funds from the American Recovery and Reinvestment Act (ARRA, or federal stimulus money) for onetime rapid job-development programs. What follows is a snapshot of the increased and new program activities that were taking form at the time of writing. We present them as they were outlined in the application.

1. Dislocated Worker Support. Eligible participants within each of the activity areas will receive support activities, including money management classes, case management assistance, personal development workshops and support group assistance. ARRA support will be used to expand the current case management contract and provide for incidental costs of the service.

2. Copycents Expansion. WRLP maintains a media production training program that enables individuals to learn basic video skills such as videography, lighting and sound. The expansion will occur in two ways. The first is to increase the number of students receiving training as well as expand the number and variety of video opportunities. Expansion will focus on increasing student involvement on video productions, including client interactions, and increasing the scope of the video production work to include supporting videos produced by students around projects they are initiating, as well as WRLP-initiated projects. ARRA support will be utilized to employ a production coordinator, who will be responsible for working with customers and students, equipment required to support the expansion and stipends to support student fieldwork. It also includes course registration costs, program supplies, and program-related travel and communication costs.

3. Electronic Records Management Training Program. WRLP will develop an electronic records management training program that will consist of classroom training, in-house training using appropriate equipment, and direct fieldwork accomplishing records management processes. Those selected for the program will complete classroom instruction, including opportunities to have hands-on experience with equipment, as well as in-the-field projects (simulated job training) for agencies that require this type of service. ARRA support will be utilized to employ a medical record project coordinator, who will be responsible for classroom and simulated job training, as well as the stipends required to support student fieldwork. It also includes course registration costs, program supplies, and program-related travel and communication costs. There will be space required to house the project.

4. Job Development/Cooperative Job Placement. This set of activities will set up and place individuals who have completed the job-training portion of the program into employment opportunities. These co-op opportunities may include video production, warehousing, sales, electronic records, or similar positions. ARRA support will be utilized to pay a placement specialist, who will arrange and monitor the co-op placements, as well as support the WRLP share of the co-op cost. There also will be program supplies, and program-related travel and communication costs that are related to these activities.

5. Basic Needs Distribution System. This set of activities will obtain, prepare, and provide for distribution of a wide range of basic need products. These products are household products that are used daily but cannot be purchased with food stamps. Examples of these products include toilet paper, diapers, personal hygiene products, cleaning products, and toiletries. These products are donated to WRLP but must be shipped from the donor to WRLP, inspected for usability, prepared for distribution and packaged. Products will be distributed to agencies that work with individuals who are affected by employment reduction and dislocations. Dislocated workers will be given priority in assisting with the preparation project and may also receive casework assistance as part of the project design. A community network will be used to coordinate with agencies. This project is also connected to product recycling. Much of the donated product, while new, requires processing in order to be usable. Having the capacity to process will keep the product out of the solid waste system. ARRA support will be utilized to provide for a production leader who will supervise the preparation process, transportation cost to get the product from the donor to WRLP, stipend cost for those assisting with product preparation, and space cost for processing and storage. There also will be program supplies and program-related travel and communication costs that are related to these activities.

6. Foreclosure Prevention Assistance. This set of activities will provide financial counseling, homeowner counseling, and transitional assistance to maintain occupancy. This activity will be subcontracted to an agency(ies) who already has the expertise to provide this needed service. ARRA support will be utilized to pay for the required counseling, financial management classes if required, and transitional assistance to maintain occupancy.

7. Entrepreneurial Development. This set of activities will provide counseling and microloans to assist dislocated workers develop their own business enterprises. This activity will be subcontracted to an agency(ies) who already has the expertise to provide this needed service. ARRA support will be utilized to pay for the required counseling, business development classes if required, and microloans to help "seed" new enterprises as a source of matching dollars.

8. Construction Skills Training. The program will work in partnership with existing construction training programs by providing training in specific construction-related skills and the opportunity to obtain hands-on training on construction sites. ARRA support will be utilized to pay for stipend assistance to qualified individuals. The specific construction skill training would be conducted by the training partner, and the training costs would be absorbed by other funding sources.

APPENDIX 2

Angelia Ijames's Graduation Speech for the First Class of the Welfare Reform Liaison Project, 1999

Good evening, ladies and gentlemen,

It is with great honor and distinct pleasure that I stand before you on this blessed day. My name is Angelia Ijames. I am the single parent of three children. I am a graduate of the first class given by the Welfare Reform Liaison Project, Inc. Let me begin there. When I came to Welfare Reform Liaison Project over one year ago, I came looking only to get some computer skills—what I received was a second chance. I was a welfare recipient with diminishing dreams and fading hope. I heard someone once compare living in poverty to being in prison. The fight against slavery took the shackles off of our feet, but poverty issues place the shackles on our mind. Living in the projects, people selling drugs on the street corners, alcohol being sold in every corner store. The same corner store that accepts all of the food stamps and money that come their way, but yet there is no respect, bullets piercing the nights, and more brothers in prison than walking the street. . . . I came to Welfare Reform tired of not being able to see the forest for the trees.

What I received from Welfare Reform is more than I can put into words. The compassion, respect, honor, uplifting kind words of encouragement and support I was shown provided me with a foundation to build upon. People gathered together to support people who want to make a change. Reverend Cleveland is always straightforward and bold with the Truth. His sharing of his own life experiences and struggles renewed my hope for tomorrow. I figured if God can do it for him, then I know he can do it for me. The staff of WRLP provided me with role models and mentors as well as accountability. During the class I had the opportunity to take a good look at myself and identify some of the things that have held me back. Things such as attitude, fear of the unknown, comfort zone, bad habits, etc. Each day that I went to class, I received a blessing. There were times it was material, sometimes inspirational, always educational and spiritual. It was just what I needed, so I made my main goal to not miss a day of getting what God has for me. New knowledge, a clearer understanding of my life, and a paradigm shift are the greatest gifts that I received from God working through Welfare Reform Liaison Project.

Once I completed the class, my first goal was met. I then had to face some issues that I was aware of but of instead of dealing with them, I was operating in denial. I can recall the day I made that phone call to Mrs. Nancy and she told me to come on over. I entered the office with a tear-stained face; once I entered her office she took my hands in hers and began to pray over the situation. I can truthfully say that the situation has not been the same since that day. Reverend Cleveland came in later and his concern was while I deal with my situation, what was I going to do in the meantime. He said you do not need to go back to doing the same old things. Instead I began volunteering my time at WRLP. Although I was not physically getting paid, my heart and mind were being paid in full. Reverend Cleveland had told me that someone was going to donate a vehicle to the program and he was interested in donating it to me. I was using my mother's vehicle at the time. Once I went to apply for a job, the way was already made—I got a job. About one month later Mrs. Nancy came to my apartment to ask me if I was still in need of transportation. God was blessing.

A week later changes started to occur on the job, the number of employees had been cut to less than half, and management was requesting that we come in late or leave early. This was not what I wanted to hear. I realized that I needed to look for another job. I then signed on with a temp agency to get some work. I was just determined that I was going to work. After completing the temporary job assignment, my son became ill and was diagnosed with diabetes. I began to worry at that point, because I was running back and forth to doctors and classes to get the diabetes under control. I was afraid of being where I just came from—welfare. At this time I received a letter in the mail from WRLP offering a continuation of paid job training. This is what I'm talking about, just when you need them, they are right there for you. I worked as receptionist for about nine weeks; I loved my job and looked forward to going to work each day. Then the day came that Reverend Cleveland asked me to go work somewhere else. He almost had to push me out the door, because I grew comfortable right where I was. I went to United Way of Greater Greensboro on May 1, 2000, as a staff trainee being paid by Welfare Reform Liaison Project, Inc. On June 5, 2001, I was offered a position with United Way as an administrative assistant making over $20,000 a year. I have full benefits including paid observed holidays, health insurance, vision care, and paid week vacation after six months of employment. I sometimes find it rather ironic that God took a plain old country girl and placed her in the midst of lead executives and volunteers over the top fifty contributing businesses in Greensboro, planning and allocating millions of dollars to building strong community. Today, before closing I would like to share with you:

MO' BETTA MOTIVATION

Sometimes you can block your blessings because of past emotional wounds, disappointments, limited thinking and small faith. Sometimes a new love, friendship, opportunities and blessings can show up in your life And you don't see them or receive them because of past hurts, you're either afraid, feel unworthy or got used to being without. For example, I recall frying some chicken on a hot summer day while pregnant with my son. The hot grease popped and burned my chest badly. I didn't fry chicken for twenty years because in my mind, frying chicken equals pain. I overlearned an experience. The scar has since healed, but apparently the emotional scar lasted a long time in my mind. You could do the same thing too. Fail a test, betrayal or abandonment in a relationship, overlooked for a promotion, bitter divorce, credit not approved, et cetera . . . the rejection and pain could cause you to overlearn an experience. Then you find yourself saying, "I'll never love or trust again . . . I'll never graduate . . . I'll never have a home . . . I'll never lose weight . . . I can't win." These feelings and thoughts close your heart and mind to receiving new love and new experiences of success and fulfillment. Who or what has "burned" you badly? What and who is showing up in your life right now? What negative experienced has caused you to "overlearn" and take it to the extreme. Don't be afraid. Stop talking yourself out of a blessing. You are worthy. Life is a risk. There are no guarantees. But you are guaranteed to continue living in lack and stagnation until you're ready to grow out of your comfort zone. Break the yoke of resistance, fear and procrastination. Every day miracles happen. Every day that you have breath in your body is a new beginning. Live your life expecting miracles. Live your life knowing you are blessed and that you are a blessing to others. The book of Isaiah 52 states "Awake, clothe yourself with strength, put on garments of splendor, shake off your dust and rise up, free yourself from the chains." —*Setaria W. Rivers*

Believe and Succeed

APPENDIX 3

Smoke-and-Mirrors Grant

This grant application, written in 1998 by Welfare Reform Liaison Project when it was a young and inexperienced organization, has been reproduced here with all of its idiosyncrasies of spelling and punctuation, grammar and syntax, which fortunately were not a barrier to getting funded. We have not included the appendices to the grant, except for appendix C, a brief explanation of the 1996 Welfare Reform Act.

Faith Community Information and Connection Program:
By Welfare Reform Liaison Project

The survival of "many" is dependent upon the actions and responses of "a few" who are currently "sounding the alarm".

A Proposal Submitted to the Joseph M. Bryan Foundation Grant Program for Health and Human Services Grant—United Way of Greater Greensboro

Rev. Odell Cleveland
Executive Director
Welfare Reform Liaison Project
1301 Alamance Church Road
Greensboro, North Carolina 27406

May 18, 1998

Ms. Antonia Monk Reaves
Bryan Foundation Grant Program
United Way of Greater Greensboro
PO Box 14998
Greensboro, NC 27415-4998

Dear Ms. Reaves:

The Welfare Reform Liaison Project is a new nonprofit organization housed in Mount Zion Baptist Church. It emerged out of a concern for what will happen this August when some women will no longer be eligible to receive cash assistance if they don't have a job. Welfare Reform Liaison Project will help the needy through emergency assistance, food distribution, clothing distribution, education, and other support programs.

Before we start actual services we will need to know who is doing what in service provision in the local churches so those churches can be tapped for help. Since other agencies would like to have a realistic picture of the range of help being offered by area churches, especially in the African American community, Welfare Reform Liaison Project is proposing to assess the faith community's outreach programs which benefit the needy. This project will serve as a brokerage of information to community agencies and churches to facilitate cooperation and efficiency of delivery of services. Welfare Reform Liaison Project is requesting $25,000 for this program.

We hope you look favorably upon our assessment program.

In His Service,
Minister Odell Cleveland, Executive Director

GRANT PROJECT NARRATIVE

A. SYSTEM FRAGMENTATION

This project will address issues that inhibit service effectiveness, especially system fragmentation, and lack of communication between agencies and the faith community.

The new welfare reform has already put demands on the faith community and will undoubtedly continue to do so for some time to come. In the last nine years, Mount Zion Baptist Church, Inc. out of which Welfare Reform Liaison Project emerged, has distributed over $402,574 in cash alone, to help families avoid eviction from their houses, help elderly people pay for much needed prescriptions, and help other families keep electricity, to cite but 3 of the many things we have done with our Emergency Assistance Ministry (See Appendix A).

Strikingly, over the last six years, 75% of the help went to people who were not members of Mount Zion (See Appendix B). Many of these individuals were referred to Mount Zion from other local community agencies such as: The Department of Social Services Emergency Assistance Program, Project Independence, Community Action, other Urban Ministry Programs, Work First, and Greensboro Housing Coalition, to name a few programs. Do other churches have resources? No one knows!

As the new welfare reform takes hold in the Greensboro community, we are going to have to pull all of our resources in to help people who lose their support from the public system (See Appendix C for a short synopsis of the new welfare reform law). At this particular time, nobody knows what the churches are doing and nobody knows what the churches can do. *This is system fragmentation!* As people realize that they can no longer go to the public agencies, they are going to have to spend an absorbing amount of time and energy, (and they may fail), trying to find some immediate help.

Welfare Reform Liaison Project is going to bring together the fragmented pieces of services in the faith community and broker some information about all of those services. The project will assess what the faith community is doing and is capable of doing. In the next several years, as welfare reform eliminates people from the roles, (whether they have jobs or not), we will hear more requests for help at Mount Zion and throughout the white and black faith community (See Appendix D). Mount Zion and most others are not prepared for the expected increase in demands for emergency assistance.

B. SPECIFIC NEED

The specific need that is being addressed is this: where are the women and children who are no longer eligible for services under Work First going to get help when they are hungry, they don't have any clothes, they don't have a place to stay when traditional places like Urban Ministry are full, and they don't know where to turn? Presently they are 1,009 families in Guilford county receiving TANF monies, come August we are going to have our first 29 families who are no longer eligible to receive cash assistance. What will happen to these families? Even if the economy remains strong, by the end of the year one hundred people won't have jobs nor be eligible for services. One hundred mothers and two hundred kids. Again, we must ask the question: What will happen to these families?

Ironically, we have over 431 churches in Greensboro, 160 of which are in the black community. How many offer social services? Community agencies are going to look to the faith community for help. This project will be able to say specifically who is doing what. Right now the system is fragmented and cannot meet expected needs. We will eliminate fragmentation by facilitating cooperation and efficiency of delivery of services. This will help kids and moms.

C. SPECIFIC POPULATION SERVED

The Welfare Reform Liaison Project ultimately is going to provide services to women by teaching them basic skills, GED classes, budgeting, decision making, stress management, and help with financial resources. We will also, help connect women to other resources and people in the community and churches that will provide services such as childcare, transportation, training, drug treatment, access to job networks, and coordination with other agencies. We cannot succeed without knowing who is doing what in the faith community.

The typical TANF (welfare) family has a 29-year old mother with two children. Some of these women have never held a full-time job, nor have a high school diploma or even basic reading and writing skills. Many do not own a car or have a driver's license. Others have a problem with drugs or alcohol. Finally, many of these families include children who are too young to be left alone when their mothers leave home to go to work.

There are two tiers of churches in the community that we will be working with. I will try to assess what the capacity is of the white churches that are in the suburbs that really aren't close to many of the problems nor the neighborhoods where many of the welfare reform recipients live. So we will try to figure out what they are doing or have the capacity or desire to contribute. With the 160 or so of the African American Churches, we would also want to assess them, but they are much closer to the neighborhoods that many of these women live in the Greensboro area. So we will look to them for direct services.

D. ACTIVITIES AND TIMETABLE

We will have five distinct project activities. The first of which will be to assemble a community advisory group of those people in social services, people who have been or currently a recipient of Work First services, and members of the faith community. We will use them as people who can:

1. Help us shape the questions that we need to ask of the various religious leaders and the providers of services in the faith and nonprofit communities so that we can understand the gaps in services from people who are both recipients and delivers of service.

2. Gather the information from our advisory committee and develop a questionnaire that will enable us to get information about the types of services that the religious congregations are offering on their premises and the kinds of other help that they are doing for agencies in the community.

3. Ask where these congregations feel that they can offer more services. Is it in helping in the community? Is it through providing volunteers? Is it through money? Is it through use of their facilities to broker other kinds of programs?

The *second* project activity is to develop a questionnaire based on the information from the advisory group.

The *third* project activity is to have the project director personally go around to as many churches as possible to learn first hand what they are doing. This will allow him to meet the chief contact people so that when we do send out the survey, which will take them time to answer and gather information resources. They will be answering a person who has personally asked them to do it.

The *fourth* project activity is to assess the information gathered from the survey and to bring it back to my advisory group to determine it's meaning. Next, we will put this information into a form where it can be used by the United Way, other churches, DSS and Urban Ministry. This information will help cut down on some of the fragmentation and give us a basis upon which to build our other programs.

The *fifth* project activity would be to hold a community conference of Work First recipients, religious leaders, community agencies, and DSS workers. The goal of this conference will be to talk about what the social service community is lacking, what the church community has, and what both systems need to effectively address the problems that are going to be faced by women who no longer have support, nor have a job.

E. PROCEDURE

Since our target population is the broader social service community that is fragmented, we are going to try to reconnect or interconnect the faith community with the broader social service community in order to help welfare recipients. We will follow the recommendations of the community advisory group, and we plan to use the services of Fasihuddin Ahmed, Ph.D. (Director of Carolina Evaluation Research Center), to conduct an examination of local religious social services. We will have a conference at the end of this process to make sure that the information gets into the hands of the people who can then use it to fix fragmentation. United Way In Touch Referral, Urban Ministry, Pulpit Forum Of Greensboro, Goodwill Industries, Work First, Greensboro Housing Authority, City Government, and other local agencies come to mind. Our final report will outline what the *churches can* and *can't do* in terms of service delivery.

The social services community and the religious community will serve as the target population. When these connections are made as a result of this project, we will certainly provide better services to the women and children that are affected by this new policy.

F. RELATIONSHIP BETWEEN EXISTING PROGRAMS

There are no similar projects in the community. We have received support letters from Greensboro Urban Ministry, Pulpit Forum Of Greensboro, Catholic Social Services, and First Presbyterian Church stating that this is an issue that has long needed attention. Leaders know that they will probably be called upon many times to give help when their resources are stretched. This information will help them. We are currently working with the DSS and have Ms. Barbara Isreal (Work First) on our board of directors to ensure that there is coordination, but DSS does not have the information about the faith community. We have also met with Ms. Phyllis Latta (Interim Director of DSS) to inform her of what we are doing. I see absolutely no overlap. We are complementary to what others are doing. Our goal is to complement all of the human service agencies in Greensboro.

G. AGENCY'S CAPABILITY

The welfare Reform Liaison Project has the full backing and complementary support of Mount Zion Baptist Church. The church has contributed the salary of the director to this project, office space, and a pool of volunteers, who will eventually work in the non-technical part of this program. Rev. Odell Cleveland (project director) has served as an associate minister. He knows the church community, and was raised by a single divorced mother with four kids. His personal experiences in overcoming the many obstacles that usually accompany poverty. Rev. Cleveland is familiar with many of the smaller African American churches, very difficult arena to do assessment of service. Yet many of the Work First recipients are surrounded by those churches.

H. MEASURABLE PROJECT OUTCOMES

We are going to do the best that we possibly can to find out what are the number of services that already exist within Greensboro churches, and how to make those services accessible to those individuals who are no longer eligible for cash assistance. We are going to assess the space availability in the community for programs, the potential for financial contributions from the faith community, and other kinds of resources that might be used to help put women back on their feet. There are over 431 churches in this community that we will contact. We will have a service grid that tells the Department of Social Services, Greensboro Urban Ministry, and other emergency agencies, what the church is doing, what it wants to do, and who to contact.

This information will be essential in short term crises and long term projects and programs. The information will allow us the ability to know which churches will get involved in the future, which churches are running at capacity now, and which churches do not want to get involved at all. We must always remember that church activities are voluntary.

I. PROJECT ACCOUNTABILITY

Project accountability will be maintained in four ways: (1) An advisory committee that will be constantly watching and giving advise on how to get the best information possible from the faith community and feed it back into the social service community. (2) Hiring a professional evaluator so that we get the most accurate and appropriate information so that the community will be responding to fair information and not manufactured information. (3) Voluntary consultation and support from professionals in the Universities, who have been voluntary consultants to this project. (4) A conference that brings the community together to plan next steps.

J. FUNDS

Ten thousand dollars will be used to pay Dr. Ahmed from the Carolina Evaluation Research Center for his services; $5,500 will be used to create a web-page and list server for the community; $3,000 will be used for conference, materials, lunches and putting together reports; $6,000 will be used for part time secretarial support and $500 will be used for travel.

K. OTHER FUNDS

Mount Zion Baptist Church has contributed over $99,600 in the form of the Project Director's salary, communication, volunteers, equipment (fax, copier), office furniture, office space, and utilities. This is what is committed to the total program. In order to be successful we will need this information because there is no way that Welfare Reform Liaison Project can serve all of the people who will fall off of welfare, without information about what other churches are doing. In this way, we can coordinate and broker with the faith community.

In answering the question, why are additional funds not available from the agency /department's overall budget? We feel that $99,600 from Mount Zion is a very, very substantial commitment for a brand new project. We believe that it is very important for us to start this project with the commitment from a local funding agency like the United Way, because it will make our application stronger to other funding sources in the area, like the Z. Smith Reynolds Foundation, or other larger foundations like the Bryan foundation which do fund projects across the state. We will be more credible if we show that we have been supported by the local community. This is our first project and this is why we are starting this way.

PROGRAM TIMELINE

May 1998—Develop funding plans

June 1998—Assemble a community advisory committee

July 1998—Hire part-time clerical assistant

July 1998—Work with Dr. Ahmed and community advisory committee

July 1998–October 1998—Meet with 250 leaders of Greensboro faith community to inform them of the future service assessment

October 1998—Assess interviews with leaders

October 1998—Implement survey (Black Churches)

November 1998—Implement survey (White Churches)

December 1998—Analyze information and plan conference

January 1999—Complete analysis

February 1999—Reassemble advisory committee

March 1999—Take advisory committee's recommendations

April 1999—Develop final report

May 1999—Hold conference

BUDGET NARRATIVE

The Welfare Reform Liaison Project's budget of $193,140 was prepared using management's best estimate of "needs" vs. "capacity" and standard/estimates for various cost categories. Welfare Reform Liaison project is a new, important project which needs to go beyond the volunteer support that has sustained it so far. We are taking our concerns to the community.

Disturbed that the federal welfare bill of 1996 would push a million more children into poverty, Peter Edelman quit his Clinton Administration post with this reminder: "We are not just talking policy, we are talking values." The value of "personal responsibility" dominated framing of welfare reform plans. Mount Zion Baptist Church of Greensboro, Inc. now moves to lift the moral value of "community responsibility"—mercy plus justice—to balance welfare reform implementation. Welfare Reform Liaison Project is another catalytic step in Mount Zion's long tradition of social justice work. Welfare Reform Liaison Project gives faith groups the tools to exercise their values of compassion and prophetic justice in concrete ways. We will help faith-based groups understand welfare reform, so they can both (1) address individual needs of Work First families and (2) more skillfully call for economic policies fair to all families in a time of increasing wealth disparities and job flight due to globalization and deindustrialization. It is important for policymakers to have realistic and sober feedback on the capacity of the faith community to bear hoped-for safety net functions as government cuts $54 billion from Food Stamps, Social Security disability, nutrition programs, and ends entitlements to cash benefits.

CONTRIBUTIONS

The local business community will be asked to help build the financial foundation for this joint community effort. Implement a strong marketing campaign that targets the potential donors.

GRANTS

Identify the foundations that historically have been powerful allies to the black church. Lilly Endowment ($3.8 billion) and the Ford Foundation ($6.6 billion), both of which make grants to study the social role of black churches and to enhance their capacity to deliver services.

PROGRAM WORKSHOPS

These are workshop that will help design individual faith groups design and/or implement their own social services delivery system. This study will allow the participants to learn their true capacity to provide services and establish a resource bank.

ANNUAL CHARITY BANQUET

The banquet will help Welfare Reform Liaison Project raise money to assist lower-income families. Tickets for Welfare Reform Liaison Project's annual banquet will cost $30.00 per person or $200.00 for a table of eight. Information: 336-273-7930

STAFFING

To prepare for the expected increases in assistance, we feel that a full-time staff must be in place to properly run Welfare Reform Liaison Project's programs. FY 98 staffing levels will consist of three (3) full time employees.

WAGES AND SALARY

Estimated wage and salary program are currently under study to assure market value. A four percent merit increase will be given at the end of each year, if evaluations deem such is appropriate.

FRINGE BENEFTTS

The fringe benefit program will consist of health care, vacation, disability, and holidays. However initiatives to evaluate alternatives, especially with regard to health benefits, are underway, and may lead to a mid year amendment to the budget to incorporate cost savings resulting from adoption of one or more such alternatives.

CONSULTANTS

We feel that by investing in professional advice from the beginning, will prove to be cost saving in the long run. This advice will allow Welfare reform liaison project to avoid many of the costly pitfalls that hamper so many non-profits.

MATERIALS AND SUPPLIES

The staff must have the proper material to do the job that is expected of them.

COMMUNICATION

Welfare Reform Liaison Project has surveyed other organizations that perform similar functions, and concluded that our technology capabilities must be on the same level.

TRAVEL

Travel will consist of community networking and partnership building, along with conferences and training.

STAFF AND VOLUNTEER TRAINING

Training Workshops that allow them to be more efficient and productive concerning welfare reform and DSS issues.

EQUIPMENT

The proper equipment will allow everyone to reach their full potential and increase capacity.

RENT

Office space will be donated by Mount Zion Baptist Church of Greensboro, Inc.

UTILITIES

We project a cost of $100.00 per month to cover our cost.

CONFERENCE

Conference of 50 or more churches to explain welfare reform.

LIABILITY INSURANCE

This insurance will be used to cover Welfare Reform Liaison Project and its board members from any potential financial harm.

WELFARE REFORM LIAISON PROJECT
1998 PROPOSED BUDGET

	PUBLIC SUPPORT	MOUNT ZION In-kind contributions[a]
	$33,000	
Grants	$83,310	
Total	$116,310	
OTHER REVENUE		
Program workshop fees	$6,000	
Annual charity dinner	$3,000	
Total	9,000	
TOTAL PUBLIC SUPPORT AND OTHER REVENUE	$125,310	
ITEMS		
A. Personnel		
1. Salary and Wages		
Project director (100%)[a]		$43,000
Administrative assistant (100%)	$25,000	
Clerical assistant (100%)	$19,500	
Fringe benefits @ .22%	$19,250	
2. Consultants		
Project consultant (20 days at $500 per day)	$10,000	
Bookkeeper/incorporation[a]		$2,500
Lawyers	$1,000	
Personnel subtotal	$74,750	$45,000
B. Non-Personnel		
1. Materials and Supplies		
Office supplies	$2,100	
Printing newsletters	$1,500	
Postage and mailing	$1,100	
Outreach ministry booklet	$1,000	
Educational materials	$2,200	

2. Communications		
Telephone, computer lines		$1700
Network connection: $20/month)	$240	
Web hosting: $50/month	$600	
Reg. domain name	$100	
Web page/e-mail setup	$200	
Hardware setup	$200	
Database setup	$200	
3. Travel		
Community resource development	$1,150	
4. Staff and volunteer training	$1,500	
5. Volunteer contributions[a]		$40,500
(30 volunteers giving 150 hours each		
[4,500 hours] per year at $9 per hour		$40,500
6. Equipment		
Phone, fax, answering machine	$600	
2 computers and printers[a]	$2,000	$1,500
1 scanner	$300	
Copier + maint. agreement	$1,900	
Office furniture[a]		$2,000
7. Rent (3-room office, $600/month)[a]		$7,200
8. Utilities ($100/month)[a]		$1,200
Nonpersonnel subtotal	$16,890	$54,100
C. Conference (Churches)		
1 per year, co-sponsored	$700	
D. Liability Insurance		
Board of Directors	$1,200	
Total	**$93,540**	**$99,600**
Total Program Cost		**$193,140**

[a]Indicates what Mount Zion Baptist Church of Greensboro will contribute to the project.

APPENDIX C
1996 WELFARE REFORM ACT

On August 22, President Clinton signed into law "The Personal Responsibility and Work Opportunity Reconciliation act of 1996 (P.L. 104-193)," effectively "ending welfare as we know it." The new legislation marks the end of the original foundation of the U.S. public welfare system, Aid to Families with Dependent Children (AFDC), and announces the advent of its replacement, Temporary Assistance for Needy Families (TANF). The new program differs significantly from the old. AFDC was an open-ended entitlement program—poor families with demonstrated need had a *right* to AFDC payments regardless of behavior, employment history, or time spent on welfare. In sharp contrast, TANF is a block-grant program with provisional benefits limited to five years (or less at state option). Welfare is no longer guaranteed to poor families, but contingent upon compliance with a state's definition of acceptable behavior.

Source: U.S. Department of Health & Human Services, *Welfare Reform. 1996. Frequently Asked Questions: What Is the New Welfare Reform Bill Actually and What Is It All About?* Washington, D.C.: U.S. Department of Health & Human Services.

GREENSBORO
URBAN
MINISTRY
May 12, 1998

Ms. Antonia Monk Reaves
Bryan Foundation Grant Program
United Way of Greater Greensboro
P.O. Box 14998
Greensboro, N.C. 27415-4998

Dear Antonia:

I am writing in support of the Welfare Reform Liaison Project's proposal to access the faith community's outreach programs which benefit the needy. This information will be used as a resource for faith and non-profit human service agencies and congregations to better coordinate their efforts in serving the Greater Greensboro community. A goal of this assessment is to facilitate cooperation and efficiency of delivery of services. Too many congregations are doing very valuable work in helping those in crisis; unfortunately, it is being done in isolation. In the next several years, as welfare reform eliminates people from the roles, (whether they have jobs or not), we will hear more requests .for help throughout the white and black faith community. Congregations are not prepared for the expected increase in demands for our emergency assistance. We, the faith community, must learn to do a much better job of collaboration and coordination. To fail in doing this will result in the inefficient use of most valuable resources.

I feel that this is an issue that has long needed attention. I have been very impressed with the process of assessing the needs of the community that have been carried out of the past several months by Rev. Odell Cleveland, a minister at Mt. Zion Baptist Church, and the Welfare Reform Liaison Project. I look forward to continue working with him, the Liaison Project, and the entire religious community as we face this exciting challenge. I hope you will fully fund this most vital effort that comes at such a crucial time in the history of human welfare.

Rev. Mike Aiken Executive Director

APPENDIX 4

In-Kind Contributions
by Ronald Fowler and Amy Henchey

From *http://www.irs.gov/pub/irs-tege/eotopice94.pdf*

1. INTRODUCTION

Today's technology informs the public about the political, social, and economic crises that plague many parts of our world. Americans are deluged with reports on starving adults, children, and families, and are motivated to assist them by providing food, medical supplies and shelter. As a result, numerous prepared and perishable food rescue programs have come into existence. Many of these organizations seek contributions of property sometimes referred to as "in-kind" contributions—from businesses, which they in turn distribute to individuals needing assistance. Sometimes, too, a soliciting organization acts as an intermediary between a business having property to donate and IRC 501(c)(3) organizations whose charitable programs involve assisting needy individuals.

While undoubtedly an overwhelming majority of these organizations serve real charitable needs, the Service is aware of organizations that take advantage of donors' good intentions and tax provisions designed to provide an incentive for in-kind donations. In dealing with "problem" organizations that solicit in-kind contributions, the Service must perform a delicate balancing act. In the view of some, food service companies are being discouraged from instituting donations of food or increasing existing donations by overly restrictive interpretation of the tax law. Part of that law, in particular IRC 170(e)(3), was enacted to provide an incentive to donate. In applying relevant tax law provisions, however, the Service must be mindful not only of the policy of encouraging donations of property used to assist needy individuals, but also of the need to prevent this well-intended provision's use for fraudulent purposes.

This article will discuss in-kind contributions, particularly those which may come within the enhanced deduction provisions in IRC 170(e)(3). It will focus on two areas in which abuses have come to light—valuation of donated goods and actual use of donated goods in programs serving the needy.

2. OVERVIEW OF IRC 170(E)(1)

To understand the enhanced deduction provisions in IRC 170(e)(3), one must first examine the basic rules governing contributions of ordinary income and capital gain property contained in IRC 170(e)(1).

Generally, individuals and corporations can deduct charitable contributions under IRC 170(a)(1). For contributions of property, the amount of the deduction is generally the fair market value of the donated property at the time of donation. See Reg. 1.170A-1(c)(1). Under IRC 170(e)(1), however, the fair market value must be reduced by the amount of gain that would not be long-term capital gain if the property had been sold by the donor at the property's fair market value (determined at the time of the contribution). Under this rule, deductions for donated inventory are limited to the property's basis (generally its cost), where the fair market value exceeds the basis.

The rationale for this reduction provision lies in the fact that a business's sale of inventory property produces ordinary income. The legislative history of the provision makes this clear. IRC 170(e)(1)(A) was added by the 1969 Tax Reform Act. The Senate Finance Committee explained the reasons for enacting this section, as follows:

[I]n some cases it actually is possible for a taxpayer to realize a greater after-tax profit by making a gift of appreciated property than by selling the property, paying the tax on the gain and keeping the proceeds. This is true in the case of gifts of appreciated property which would result in ordinary income if sold, when the taxpayer is at a high marginal tax bracket and the cost basis for the ordinary income property is not a substantial percentage of the fair market value. For example, a taxpayer in the 70 percent tax bracket could make a gift of $100 of inventory ($50 cost basis) and save $105 in taxes (70 percent of the $50 gain if sold, or $35, plus 70 percent of the $100 fair market value of the inventory, or $70). The committee does not believe that the charitable contributions deduction was intended to provide greater—or even nearly as great tax benefits in the case of gifts of property than would be realized if the property were sold and the proceeds were retained by the taxpayer. In cases where the tax savings is so large, it is not clear how much charitable motivation actually remains. It appears that the Government, in fact, is almost the sole contributor to the charity. Moreover, an unwarranted tax benefit is allowed these taxpayers, who usually are in the very high income brackets. The committee, therefore, considers it appropriate to narrow the application of the tax advantages in the case of gifts of certain appreciated property. S. Rep. No. 552, 91st Cong., 1st Sess. 80 (1969).

3. THE IRC 170(E)(3) EXCEPTION

A. GENERAL REQUIREMENTS

The basis standard for deduction of contributions of inventory and similar property came under heavy fire even at the outset, according to 1976 public hearings on general tax reform before the House Committee on Ways and Means. Charitable organizations complained that donors of inventory discontinued contributions rather than deal with the restrictions. A substantial amount of evidence was presented to show that charitable organizations most affected by IRC 170(e) were those involved in distributing food, medicine, clothing, and other basic necessities. As a result, the Tax Reform Act of 1976 added IRC 170(e)(3), effective for contributions made after October 4, 1976. In March 1980, proposed regulations were published; final regulations were adopted incorporating certain changes effective January 29, 1982. IRC 170(e)(3) provides an exception to the basis standard and gives prospective donors business reasons to consider making charitable donations of inventory. If a corporation, other than an S corporation, contributes section 1221(1) or (2) property, it may deduct an amount exceeding the property's basis (determined in accordance with Reg. 1.170A-4A(c)(2)).

To be eligible to receive deductions qualifying under IRC 170(e)(3), the donee must be an IRC 501(c)(3) organization and a public charity or a private operating foundation. Of course, other requirements for deductibility under IRC 170(c)(2) must be met. Thus, the contribution must be to or for the use of a domestic organization. See Rev. Rul. 63-252, 1963-2 C.B. 101; and Rev. Rul. 66-79, 1966-1 C.B. 48, regarding the use of "conduit" organizations for foreign charities.

To receive the enhanced deduction, four requirements must be met:

(1) Donated property must be used solely for the care of the ill, the needy, or infants, and in a manner related to the donee's exempt purpose. IRC 170(e)(3)(A)(i); Reg. 1.170A-4A(b)(2). A third party may not use the property unless that use is incidental to the primary use of caring for the ill, needy, or infants. Reg. 1.170A-4A(b)(2)(ii).

(2) Donated property cannot be transferred by the donee in exchange for money, other property, or services. IRC170(e)(3)(A)(ii); Reg. 1.170A-4A(b)(3).

(3) The donee must furnish a written statement to the donor that the above requirements will be met. IRC 170(e)(3)(A)(iii); Reg. 1.170A-4A(b)(4).

(4) The property must satisfy certain requirements of the Federal Food, Drug and Cosmetic Act (if applicable). Compliance is required not only for the time the contribution is made, but for the 180 day period preceding the contribution as well. IRC 170(e)(3)(A)(iv); Reg. 1.170A-4A(b)(5).

To ascertain the deduction amount, start with the fair market value of the donated inventory property, less one-half the amount of the reduction computed under IRC 170(e)(1) (i.e., the unrealized appreciation). The resulting amount must be reduced by any amount exceeding twice the property's basis. IRC 170(e)(3)(B). Reg. 1.170A-4A(c)(4) illustrates how the required formula is applied:

Example (1). During 1978 corporation X, a calendar year taxpayer, makes a qualified contribution of women's coats which was [inventory] property. The fair market value of the property at the date of contribution is $1,000, and the basis of the property is $200. The amount of the charitable contribution which would be taken into account under section 170(a) is the fair market value ($1,000). The amount of gain which would not have been long-term capital gain if the property had been sold is $800 ($1,000 – $200). The amount of the contribution is reduced by one-half the amount which would not have been capital gain if the property had been sold. **$800/2 = $400**

After this reduction, the amount of the contribution which may be taken into account is $600 ($1,000 – $400). A second reduction is made in the amount of the charitable contribution because this amount (as first reduced to $600) is more than $400 which is an amount equal to twice the basis of the property. The amount of the further reduction is $200 [$600 – (2 x $200)], and the amount of the contribution as finally reduced is $400 [$1,000 – ($400 + $200)]. . . .

For the donor to claim the enhanced deduction, donor and donee must observe certain formalities. Reg. 1.170A-4A(b)(4) imposes an affirmative obligation on the donee to provide the donor with a written statement containing the following:

(1) A description of the contributed property, including the date of its receipt;

(2) A statement that the property will be used in compliance with the requirements of IRC 170(e)(3);

(3) A statement that the donee is an organization recognized as exempt from federal income tax under IRC 501(c)(3); and

(4) A statement that adequate books and records will be maintained and made available to the Service upon request.

Where the value of donated goods exceeds $5,000, the donee must also acknowledge the contribution on Form 8283 (Noncash Charitable Contributions), Reg. 1.170A-13(b); and file Form 8282 (Donee Information Return) if it disposes of contributed property valued at more than $500 for which it received Form 8283 (IRC 6050L and Reg. 1.6050L-1). Form 8282 is not required, however, where the donee consumes or distributes the property in furtherance of its exempt purposes. Reg. 1.6050L-1(a)(3). Reg. 1.6050L-1(c) states that IRC 6050L also applies to certain successor donees.

As noted above, most concerns the Service may have about the propriety of allowing an enhanced deduction in a particular case fall into two areas: 1) demonstrating that the property will be used for the care of the ill, needy, or infants, and in a manner consistent with the donee's exempt purpose, and 2) establishing the fair market value of the donated property.

DEFINITION OF CARE OF THE ILL, NEEDY, OR INFANTS

The first major issue under IRC 170(e)(3) is whether the donee's use of property is related to its exempt purposes, and "solely for the care of the ill, the needy, or infants." Reg. 1.170A-4A(b)(2)(ii) defines relevant terms. Reg. 1.170A-4A(b)(2)(ii)(B) defines an "ill" person broadly as one who requires medical care within the meaning of Reg. 1.213-1(e). Under Reg. 1.170A-4A(b)(2)(ii)(C), "care" of the ill means alleviation or cure of an existing illness and includes care of the physical, mental, or emotional needs of the ill.

A "needy" person is one who lacks the necessities of life, involving physical, mental, or emotional well-being, as a result of poverty or temporary distress. Reg. 1.170A-4A(b)(2)(ii)(D). "Care" of the needy consists of alleviating or satisfying a particular need. Reg. 1.170A-4A(b)(2)(ii)(E).

Finally, an "infant" is a minor child (as determined under local law). Reg. 1.170A-4A(b)(2)(ii)(F). "Care" of an infant means performing parental functions or providing for the infant's physical, mental, and emotional needs. Reg. 1.170A-4A(b)(2)(ii)(G).

RECORD-KEEPING REQUIREMENTS

As noted above, the enhanced deduction is not available unless the donee provides a written statement affirming that certain requirements will be met, and that the donee will maintain adequate books and records concerning the donation. With regard to this record-keeping requirement, Reg. 1.170A-4A(b)(4)(i) further provides as follows:

The books and records . . . need not trace the receipt and disposition of specific items of donated property if they disclose compliance with the requirements by reference to aggregate quantities of donated property. The books and records are adequate if they reflect total amounts received and distributed (or used), and outline the procedure used for determining that the ultimate recipient of the property is an ill or needy individual or infant. However, the books and records need not reflect the names of the ultimate individual recipients or the property distributed to (or used by) each one.

Whether books and records maintained satisfy these requirements will, of course, depend on the facts and circumstances of the particular case. In PLR 8737002 (May 7, 1987), for example, a public charity maintained a log recording all distributions of books to inmates. The letter ruling concluded that maintaining the log would satisfy the record-keeping requirement.

INDIRECT ASSISTANCE

Reg. 1.170A-4A(b)(2)(ii) provides, in part, that persons other than the "ill, needy, or infants" may not use donated inventory except as incidental to primary use in the care of the ill, needy, or infants. Nevertheless, the enhanced deduction may be available where donated inventory will be used indirectly in the care of such persons. For example, in PLR 8420036 (Feb. 13, 1984), a company was permitted to take the IRC 170(e)(3) deduction where it donated copying machines to health centers, laboratories, and hospitals for use in copying patient records, health educational materials, and laboratory results.

B. INTERMEDIARY ORGANIZATIONS

The regulations contemplate that donations made to one qualified organization may be subsequently transferred to another organization, for qualifying purposes. Reg. 1.170A-4A(b)(4)(ii) imposes written statement and record-keeping requirements on subsequent transferees.

PLR 8638006 (June 13, 1986) permitted a fishing equipment business to take an enhanced deduction for donations to an intermediary fund that transferred donated property to subsequent donees. The donated property—fishing equipment—would ultimately be used in recreational programs for disadvantaged persons. Similarly, PLR 8547028 (Aug. 26, 1985) permitted the enhanced deduction for donations of property to an organization that transferred the property twice before it was ultimately used in the care of the ill, needy, and infants.

Intermediary organizations thus play a recognized and legitimate role in distributing donated inventory. The Service is aware, however, of situations where title to donated property passes through several intermediary organizations which appear to play little (if any) role in facilitating distribution of the property for qualified purposes. In such situations, the chain of transactions should be carefully examined to verify that donated property is ultimately used for qualified purposes. In addition, one may question whether that provision has been satisfied, where an intermediary organization, despite lacking either physical possession or control over donated goods, nevertheless gives a written statement purporting to comply with IRC 170(e)(3)(A)(ii) and Reg. 1.170A-4A(b)(4).

C. VALUATION OF IN-KIND CONTRIBUTIONS

In determining the proper amount of a deduction under IRC 170(e)(3), there are two pertinent questions: (1) What is the basis of the inventory and (2) What is the inventory's fair market value? As an initial matter, if the fair market value of the inventory is less than its basis, then no question under IRC 170(e) generally arises—the deduction is limited to the fair market value of the donated property, under general principles. (But see Reg. 1.170A-4A(c)(2)-(3), regarding adjustments to cost of goods sold where basis is less than fair market value.) General guidance on determining fair market value of donated property is found in the regulations. Reg. 1.170A-1(c)(2) and (3) provide as follows: . . .

(2) The fair market value is the price at which the property would change hands between a willing buyer and a willing seller, neither being under any compulsion to buy or sell and both having reasonable knowledge of relevant facts. If the contribution is made in property of a type which the taxpayer sells in the course of his business, the fair market value is the price which the taxpayer would have received if he had sold the contributed property in the usual market in which he customarily sells, at the time and place of the contribution and, in the case of a contribution of goods in quantity, in the quantity contributed. The usual market of a manufacturer or other producer consists of the wholesalers or other distributors to or through whom he customarily sells, but if he sells only at retail, the usual market consists of his retail customers.

(3) If a donor makes a charitable contribution of property, such as stock in trade, at a time when he could not reasonably have been expected to realize its usual selling price, the value of the gift is not the usual selling price but is the amount for which the quantity of property contributed would have been sold by the donor at the time of the contribution. . . .

"USUAL MARKET"

In general, the most persuasive evidence of value in the donor's "usual market" for goods would be actual sales. One way to obtain such information is to secure catalogues, brochures, or other documents that list prices of items which the donor sells in the ordinary course of business. In most situations, an appraisal is not more persuasive than documentation showing the price that buyers actually paid for similar property.

The regulation also highlights that where the donor sells property in (for example) a wholesale market, it is inappropriate to value the contribution at (for example) the property's retail sales price.

"TIME AND PLACE"

The "time" of a contribution may be of particular relevance with perishable or dated items, such as food, drugs, and agricultural products. Perishable items may have a lower market value if sold shortly before they will become spoiled, for example. In addition, a donor may be unable, practically or legally, to sell items in any market when the expiration date is close at hand or past.

Rev. Rul. 85-8, 1985-1 C.B. 59, illustrates this problem. This ruling considered donations of dated pharmaceutical inventory shortly before expiration. The donor claimed a deduction for the inventory's full retail selling price (10x dollars); at the time of the donation, however, the donor "could not reasonably have been expected to realize its usual selling price for the products due to the imminence of the expiration date after which the products could not be sold legally." Accordingly, the donor's deduction was limited to 2x dollars, the value of the products if sold at the time they were actually donated, reduced in accordance with IRC 170(e)(3). The ruling emphasizes that fair market value of donated products depends "on the facts and circumstances surrounding those particular products at that particular time."

"QUANTITY"

When considering quantity, the question arises whether fair market value is determined for each unit of property or in bulk. The regulations specifically refer to the quantity contributed, as opposed to quantities normally sold in the usual market in the ordinary course of business. Thus, the value of a quantity of goods exceeding normal retail amounts may be less than the retail value, even where the donor's "usual market" is a retail one.

The quantity contributed may also affect the determination of fair market value where the donation itself has an effect on the market for the donated property. Where the market in which the donation occurs is not large enough to absorb the quantity of goods donated, for example, a lower valuation may be appropriate.

SAFE HARBOR VALUATION FOR FOOD PRODUCT DONATIONS?

The Service has received many inquiries from organizations in the rapidly growing field of prepared and perishable food rescue programs, which distribute surplus prepared and perishable food from restaurants, hotels, and caterers to food banks, shelters, and feeding programs. According to these organizations, given questions about valuation of perishable food, food service companies are reluctant to donate because they have no assurance of the amount of the deduction that will be allowed. Thus, these organizations believe current tax laws discourage food service companies from donating food, contrary to the policy underlying IRC 170(e)(3).

The Service is currently considering various proposals by such organizations to amend the regulations to provide a "safe harbor" for valuing food donations. No decision has been made as to whether any such proposals should be adopted.

4. EXEMPT STATUS CONCERNS

The availability of the enhanced charitable deduction for certain in-kind contributions may in part explain the existence of "questionable" organizations having as their purported exempt purpose the distribution of donated inventory. Consider the following hypothetical:

We Care About Hunger, Inc., is a 501(c)(3) organization created and controlled by an individual most recently employed in the direct mail industry. WCAH's stated exempt purpose is to provide humanitarian assistance to Romanian orphans. It solicits contributions of frozen food, pharmaceutical products, and infant formula, from manufacturing corporations. Many of these items are close to or past the expiration date printed on the package. WCAH also solicits books and used clothing (adult sizes). WCAH solicits financial support from the general public; its solicitation materials discuss its purpose of assisting Romanian orphans, and indicate WCAH itself provides infant formula and medical programs overseas. WCAH reports donations of inventory on its Form 990 as "contributions received" at their full retail value on the date of donation. It reports as program expenses the retail value of items transferred to other organizations. WCAH provides no assistance directly to Romanian orphans. It transfers donated inventory to other 501(c)(3) organizations, which in turn frequently transfer title to additional IRC 501(c)(3) organizations. Although WCAH receives written statements from its donees that facially comply with the requirements under IRC 170(e)(3)(A)(iii), it cannot demonstrate that donated goods are actually used to benefit Romanian orphans (or other "ill, needy, or infants"). Its transfers to other organizations are the only program expenses reported on Form 990; 100% of its financial support is paid out to the founder and members of his family as administrative and fund-raising costs. In determining if an organization that solicits and distributes in-kind contributions is exempt under IRC 501(c)(3), the Service must determine whether the organization's activities primarily further exempt purposes (Reg. 1.501(c)(3)-1(c)(1)), and whether those activities provide benefits to private individuals, other than benefits which are incidental to furthering exempt purposes (see Reg. 1.501(c)(3)-1(d)(2)). Concerns underlying IRC 501(c)(3) are similar to those underlying the enhanced deduction provision: ensuring use of donated property exclusively for charitable purposes. Thus, in considering the exemption of this kind of organization, similar considerations apply.

(a) Existence of exempt purpose: Can the organization demonstrate that its role in soliciting and distributing in-kind contributions furthers exempt purposes? The record-keeping requirements imposed by Reg. 1.170A-4A(b)(4)(i) may provide a source of information for verifying that such purposes exist. Where an organization cannot establish, through books and records, that it meets the requirements for exemption, exemption may be revoked. See, e.g., Reg. 1.6033-1(h)(2) and 1.6001-1(c), which provide record-keeping requirements for exempt organizations.

As discussed above, intermediary organizations whose activities consist of distributing in-kind contributions for use in the programs of other organizations may further charitable purposes. Care should be taken to distinguish legitimate intermediaries, such as community food banks, from organizations whose exempt purposes cannot be verified.

In the hypothetical situation outlined above, for example, WCAH's books and records do not demonstrate that in-kind contributions were ever used to benefit needy individuals. In addition, the facts provide a basis for questioning whether some items could have been used to further WCAH's stated exempt purposes. One may ask, for example, of what benefit English-language books and adult clothing could possibly be to Romanian orphans. Similarly, WCAH should be required to demonstrate that expired pharmaceutical products (for example) retained their potency at the time they were dispensed to patients, or whether the products otherwise have diminished in value, for example by being hazardous to use or consume, or illegal.

(b) Private benefit/inurement: Particularly where doubt exists as to whether in-kind contributions actually benefit needy persons, careful examination of the use of the organization's financial resources is warranted. The facts may show that the organization operates for the substantial non-exempt purpose of benefiting the business interests of related parties. See, e.g., Rev. Rul. 67-5, 1967-1 C.B. 123; International Postgraduate Medical Foundation v. Commissioner, T.C.M. 1989-36; Church by Mail, Inc. v. Commissioner, 765 F.2d 1387 (9th Cir. 1985), aff'g T.C.M. 1984-349. These interests may include for-profit fundraising organizations and entities which are paid for securing in-kind contributions (or for otherwise acquiring property) purportedly distributed as part of a charitable program.

(c) Valuation: The instructions to Form 990 require that in-kind contributions received be reported at the property's fair market value. Principles used in determining fair market value for deduction purposes may be a useful starting point; however, IRC 501(c)(3) organizations must report fair market value using generally accepted accounting principles for non-profit organizations. The applicable AICPA standard is an appendix to this article.

In some cases, an organization that takes title to property (and reports its value on Form 990 as contributions received and grants made) plays little or no role in facilitating the property's distribution for use in a program actually benefiting needy persons. Where an organization neither takes physical possession of property, nor exercises discretion or control over its re-distribution, it may not be appropriate to report any amount as contributions received/grants made on Form 990.

Where the value assigned to donated inventory for reporting purposes greatly exceeds actual fair market value, a basis for inquiring further into the legitimacy of the organization's exempt purposes may exist. In addition, penalties may be imposed for filing incomplete or incorrect returns, under IRC 6652(c). It may also be appropriate in such cases to examine whether the organization has been helping its donors inflate their deductions. See IRC 6700, 6701.

Finally, the National Office is considering whether, and in what circumstances, revocation of exempt status may be appropriate where an organization grossly overstates the value of donated inventory on Form 990. Consideration should be given to requesting technical advice if revocation on this basis is contemplated.

Over-valuation of in-kind contributions is more than a "mere" reporting problem. Over-valuation often results in significant benefits to the organization, resulting from the fact that its program expenditures, as a percentage of overall expenditures, will be greatly enhanced. It can present itself more favorably in soliciting monetary contributions from the public, and it may qualify to participate in federated fundraising drives or other programs. Form 990 is an important disclosure document for the public, state regulatory bodies, charity "watchdog" groups, and other public and private organizations. Accordingly, examination of the return should attempt to ensure that in-kind contributions are valued accurately.

5. CONCLUSION

Twenty years ago, an author writing about mail fraud schemes (E. Kahn, *Fraud: The United States Postal Inspection Service and Some of the Fools and Knaves It Has Known* 311–17 (1973)) devoted a chapter to an organization that solicited drug companies and surgical suppliers to donate inventory, purportedly to improve health facilities in the Philippines, which its promoters resold for their own profit. Upon receiving a tax exemption determination letter from the Service, the organization's promoter reportedly waved it in the air and exclaimed "Now I have a license to steal!"

Unfortunately, too many promoters of organizations involved in soliciting in-kind contributions appear to be of the same view. The IRC 501(c)(3) determination letter (and the IRC 170(e)(3) enhanced deduction) is indeed a "license to steal" if in-kind contributions are never used for exempt purposes, while promoters and related for-profit businesses are well-paid for their services. In attempting to address this apparently persistent and growing area of abuse, however, the Service must be careful that it does not frustrate Congressional policy of providing incentives for businesses to donate inventory for qualifying charitable purposes.

APPENDIX

American Institute of Certified Public Accountants, Audits of Voluntary Health and Welfare Organizations 20-21 (1974):

CHAPTER 5, DONATED MATERIAL AND SERVICES

Donated materials of significant amounts should be recorded at their fair value when received, if their omission would cause the statement of support, revenue, and expenses to be misleading and if the organization has an objective, clearly measurable basis for the value, such as proceeds from resale by the organization, price lists, or market quotations (adjusted for deterioration and obsolescence), appraisals, etc. Such recording is necessary to properly account for all transactions of the organization, as well as to obtain stewardship control over all materials received.

If the nature of the materials is such that valuations cannot be substantiated, it is doubtful that they should be recorded as contributions; used clothing received as contributions and subsequently given away might, for example, fall into this category. There is, of course, no valuation problem where donated materials are converted into cash soon after receipt, since the net cash received measures the contribution.

When donated materials are used in rendering the service provided by the organization, the cost of such materials included in the service is based on the value previously recorded for the contribution. If donated materials pass through the organization to its charitable beneficiaries and the organization merely serves as an agent for the donors, the donation normally would not be recorded as a contribution. If significant amounts are involved, the value of the materials recorded as contributions and expenditures should be clearly disclosed in the financial statements.

APPENDIX 5

Community Action Grant Rating Forms

APPLICANT NAME _____   REVIEWED BY _____

RATING FORM

PART A – REVIEW & SCORE

SECTION I – PROGRAM NARRATIVE (Maximum Points = 55)   OVERALL SCORE =

Sub-Section #	Criterion	Max Points Allowed	Total Points Earned	Comments
Sub-section 1	**Introduction.** Determine to what extent Applicant describes the organization. In the introduction, Applicants should provide a brief summary about their agency, including a brief history and mission statement. For instance, do they tell us how long they've been in operation? Is the mission clearly stated and does/could it accommodate the goal of the Community Action Program, which is to move people from poverty to self-sufficiency?	5		
Sub-section 2	**Current Operations.** Determine to what extent the Applicant provides information about its current operations. Are funding sources identified? Do they adequately describe their programs? Do they report the number of participants involved? Do they identify partnerships with local human service providers, businesses and other entities within the community? Do they indicate partnerships at the state and national levels? Is verifying documentation included in the Appendices to support the partnerships described?	10		

APPLICANT NAME _____   REVIEWED BY _____

Sub-Section #	Criterion	Max Points Allowed	Total Points Earned	Comments
Sub-section 3	**Demonstration of Effectiveness.** Determine the extent to which Applicant uses this section to show demonstrated effectiveness in obtaining positive outcomes for low-income families, in carrying out funded projects, over the past three years. Agency outcomes, successes, community changes, etc. should be included here. Were charts, graphs, annual reports or other aids referenced and supplied in the Appendices?	25		

Sub-section 4	**Transition Plan.** Determine to what extent Applicant has described how the agency would adapt if designated as the Eligible Entity. Do they offer a time line? Do they adequately illustrate a plan to change their Board (if necessary) in order to comply with CSBG requirements, which include the assurances, that:
	
	(A) the Board of Directors is composed of at least 15 members and no more than 51
	
	(B) Board members is as follows:
	
	   (i) one-third are public officials, currently holding office;
	
	   (ii) at least one third of the members are persons chosen in accordance with the democratic selection procedures that assure representatives of the poor in the area served;
		15		

APPLICANT NAME _____   REVIEWED BY _____

	(iii) the reminder of the members are officials or members of business, industry, labor, religious, welfare, education, or other major groups and interests in the community. **Please note:** For additional information, refer to the Assurance Section of the RFCD instructions document.		
	Most importantly, does the Applicant describe the democratic process they use (or will use) to recruit representatives of the poor?		
	TOTALS	**55**	

SECTION II – CERTIFICATIONS AND ASSURANCES (Maximum Points = 25)   **OVERALL SCORE =**

Sub-Section #	Criterion	Max Points Allowed	Total Points Earned	Comments
Sub-section 1	**Certifications.** Maximum points can be applied if Applicant followed instructions explicitly. To evaluate, refer to the list on page 3 of the application and the Appendices to determine if Applicant (1) completed the page, and (2) attached copies of applicable documentation in the order listed.	**10**		

APPLICANT NAME _____   REVIEWED BY _____

Sub-Section #	Criterion	Max Points Allowed	Total Points Earned	Comments
Sub-section 2	**Board of Directors.** Maximum points can be applied if Applicant followed instructions explicitly. To evaluate, refer to the list on pages 4 and 5 of the RFCD. (1) Did Applicant adequately respond to all questions? (2) Did Applicant provide a complete list of the members of the Board, including addresses? (3) Does the number of members listed match the number of seats, according to their by-laws? If not, (4) does the Applicant adequately explain the discrepancy?	**10**		
Sub-section 3	**Assurances.** Maximum points can be applied if page 7 of the RFCD Application Instructions document was completed, according to instructions.	**5**		
	TOTALS	**25**		

SECTION III– APPENDICES (Maximum Points = 20)   **OVERALL SCORE =**

Sub-Section #	Criterion	Max Points Allowed	Total Points Earned	Comments
Sub-section 1	**Appendix A.** Maximum points can be applied if Applicant followed instructions explicitly. To evaluate, refer to the list on page 3 of the RFCD and the Appendices to determine if Applicant attached copies of applicable documentation in the order listed.	**5**		
Sub-section 2	**Subsequent Appendices.** Maximum points can be applied if Applicant included at least 3 letters of support. And that, of the 3, at least one is written by a representative of a funding source.	**5**		

APPLICANT NAME _____   REVIEWED BY _____

Sub-section 3	**Subsequent Appendices.** Maximum points can be applied if additional support documents from partners (i.e. Memorandums of Agreement) at the local, state, and national levels are provided.	**5**		
Sub-section 4	**Subsequent Appendices.** This score should reflect how you assess the relevance and substance of the supportive documentation provided.	[Points that Remain]		
	TOTALS	**20**		

BONUS POINTS (Maximum Points = 10)			OVERALL SCORE =	
Sub-Section #	Criterion	Max Points Allowed	Total Points Earned	Comments
Bonus	**Outstanding or Exceptional Enhancements.** Here, you are given the opportunity to add additional quality points to reflect any exemplary documentation that significantly enhances the Applicant's candidacy for Designation.	**10**		
	TOTALS	**10**		

OVERALL SCORE FOR THIS APPLICANT

[   ]

Tally Sheet

Applying Agency	Section I				Section II			Section III				Bonus Points	TOTAL Points
	Sub-Sect. 1	Sub-Sect. 2	Sub-Sect. 3	Sub-Sect. 4	Sub-Sect. 1	Sub-Sect. 2	Sub-Sect. 3	Sub-Sect. 1	Sub-Sect. 2	Sub-Sect. 3	Sub-Sect. 4		
Maximum Points →	*5*	*10*	*25*	*15*	*10*	*10*	*5*	*5*	*5*	*5*	*5*	*10*	*110*

Ranking
From the highest scorer to the lowest, list the Applicants below.

Rank	Name of Applicant
#1	_____
#2	_____
#3	_____
#4	_____
#5	_____

Rank	Name of Applicant
#6	_____
#7	_____
#8	_____
#9	_____
#10	_____

Reviewed by _____   Date Reviewed _____

APPENDIX 6

Community Action Grant 2002

The grant application reproduced here was written in 2002 and has been reproduced here with all of its idiosyncrasies of spelling and punctuation, grammar and syntax. Again, these fortunately were not a barrier to getting funded, and we have not included the appendices.

Welfare Reform LIAISON Project, Inc.
1324 Alamance Church Road
Greensboro, North Carolina 27406
Phone: 336/691-5780   Fax: 336/691-5785
Email: wrlp@earthlink.net

January 17, 2002
Mr. Lawrence D. Wilson, Director
Office of Economic Opportunity
222 North Person Street
Raleigh, NC 27601

Dear Mr. Wilson:

Welfare Reform Liaison Project Incorporated (WRLP) is a 501(C) (3) non-profit organization located in Greensboro, NC that has established non-traditional partnerships linking private foundations, charitable groups, human service agencies, corporations, volunteers, and the faith based community to address issues of poverty. Our goal is to empower people while promoting employment and economic stability through collaboration with other agencies. WRLP, using a holistic approach, provides job-training, educational opportunities, emergency financial assistance, mentors, and job placement assistance to low income individuals in Guilford County, especially those who are in the welfare-to-work program. Participants attend a 11-week training program emphasizing a range of job readiness skills, including problem solving, working effectively with others, time management, crisis management and most importantly self esteem and confidence building. Our services provide on-the-job training in our Distribution Center, mentoring from project volunteers, job placement and case management assistance from project staff.

Our staff and Board of Directors are excited about the possibility of expanding the scope of our services, which would enable us to better serve our community. Our Board of Directors is in full agreement with making the necessary structural changes needed to be eligible for this award. The Board of Directors has approved the submission of this grant request.

Welfare Reform Liaison Project, Inc., Board Chair

Sincerely

Mrs. Lou Sua

OFFICE OF ECONOMIC OPPORTUNITY

Application For Consideration
For Designation As An Eligible
Community Services Block Grant Entity
Serving Guilford County, North Carolina

APPLICANT IDENTIFICATION

Agency Name: Welfare Reform Liaison Project, Inc.

Mailing Address: 1324 Alamance Church Road,
　　　　　　　　　Greensboro, North Carolina 27406

Administrative Office Address: 1324 Alamance Church Road,
　　　　　　　　　　　　　　　　Greensboro, North Carolina 27406

E-Mail Address: wrlp@earthlink.net

Telephone Number: (336) 691-5780

Fax Number: (336) 691-5785

Board Chairperson: Lou Sua

Executive Director: Rev. C. Odell Cleveland

Submitted to:
Lawrence D. Wilson, Director
Office of Economic Opportunity
222 North Person Street
Raleigh, North Carolina 27601
(919) 715-5850

Part I—Introduction: History and Mission of Welfare Reform Liaison Project

Our Official Mission: It shall be the mission of Welfare Reform Liaison Project, Inc. to provide those services that will enable families to move towards self-sufficiency through collaboration with the faith community, corporations, and other agencies from both the public and private sectors.

In response to the Welfare Reform Legislation of 1996, Bishop George W. Brooks, the Senior Pastor of Mt. Zion Baptist Church in Greensboro NC, selected Reverend Odell Cleveland to oversee a study of the church's emergency assistance program with an eye toward being proactive with the coming changes in welfare. The Emergency Assistance program had distributed nearly $400,000 in cash alone, mainly to non-members, during a 7-year period prior to the change in the welfare law. Welfare Reform Liaison Project emerged from the vision of Bishop Brooks, Reverend Cleveland, and the findings of that study.

After using most of 1997 to plan for the organization's development and mobilize community resources, Welfare Reform Liaison Project Incorporated (WRLP) became a 501 (c) (3) non-profit organization located in Greensboro, NC. It has established non-traditional partnerships linking private foundations, charitable groups, human service agencies, corporations, volunteers, and the faith based community to address issues of persistent poverty, which is below the surface of welfare problems. Our goal is to empower people, build community, and stimulate philanthropy, especially in minority communities, while promoting employment and economic stability through collaboration with other agencies and businesses.

WRLP, using a holistic approach, provides job-training, educational opportunities, financial assistance, mentors, and job placement assistance to low income individuals in Guilford County, especially those who are in the welfare-to-work program. Participants attend an 11-week training program emphasizing a range of job readiness skills, including problem solving, working effectively with others, time management, crisis management, and most importantly self esteem and confidence building. Some receive on-the-job training in our Distribution Center, others go into our Coop Program, and others go onto employment. They receive mentoring from project volunteers, and receive job placement assistance from project staff. We train members of the faith community how to have effective outreach service programs within their capacity and limitations. We are a community building and enhancing organization, not just a job training-center.

Part II Current Operations of Welfare Reform Liaison Project

Programs Operated.

The major goals of WRLP is (1) to assist families with special problems that prevent them from obtaining immediate employment or long-term employment and (2) develop natural support systems like family, church and community and to strengthen their capacity to help in all the ways possible. They often need a small boost, which we provide.

We have 5 programs. Keep in mind that within each program, we have several intricate components. (1) **Educational Upgrade** which takes place at our Annex. (2) **Job Training** in a sheltered environment that operates at our Distribution Center along with helping mainly African American Churches build their capacity for outreach. (3) **Coop and Job Coaching** that operates out of the Distribution Center and at job sites, and (4) **Employment** which we consider a component. While employment training is 11 weeks. We work with our students up to 18 months even while they are on the job. (5) **The Faith Summit**, which brings together our partners for a yearly conference and community planning workshops (See Appendix B, Item 1 which is a table outlining our program).

Funding Sources.

In the almost 3 years WRLP has operated its Distribution Center, we have received and distributed nearly 32 million dollars worth of new products from Gifts In Kind International. While not money in the traditional sense, merchandise comes to our Distribution Center for a small fee, and we charge an enrollment fee of $150.00 to churches and nonprofits, which allows them to receive merchandise four times a year and distribute it in their service areas. The Distribution Center is about half the size of Wal-Mart, and is a hub for our student's job training, volunteer service, and working with churches and other organizations that want to serve others. In addition, WRLP receives funds and space from Mt Zion Baptist Church. The State of North Carolina funds us through a Health and Human Services Grant that pays students stipends in our Distribution Center and Coop. The Rural Economic Development Center through a Charitable Choice Grant, allows us to help other faith-based organizations statewide develop outreach programs. The Weaver Foundation of Greensboro has given us a 5-year grant to "up-fit" and keep the Distribution Center operating. The Moses Cone/Wesley Long Health Foundation has helped us significantly for our Health Education Program (See Appendix Al Items 2-5). We have received numerous grants and donations from individuals that appear in Appendix Al Item 6-1,6-2.

Number of Participants

We are an organization that builds community. The students we serve are one set of participants, but so are their families, churches, and other support systems, including agencies and businesses that we will talk about in our section on partnerships. As a comprehensive community

service agency, we have worked with over 200 agencies and organizations to establish our focus on community. See our list of partners in Appendix Al Item 7. While we have trained nearly 120 (this includes Class 7) people directly for jobs, we have 130 churches that are part of our service mission as we have helped them develop helping and outreach ministries through our distribution program (See Appendix B Items 2 and 3) for the two letters that demonstrate this point. Over 75 volunteers have assisted us through mentoring, job training, our Faith Summit, in our administrative office and distribution center. We recently received 100, 000 children's books and partnered with the school system to distribute them (See Appendix B Item 4 for the news story). We have partnered with businesses, non-profits, and human service agencies in our Coop program. Our bi-annual Community Faith Summit brings together providers from religious organizations, nonprofit and government agencies to discuss the most effective ways to serve the poor. We have had 700 participants at our 2 summits (See Appendix B Item 5). In all we have served 50,000 people this year through the provision of goods and services.

Essentially our students get job training, which helps them develop the skills and work habits necessary to succeed. WRLP ensures the progress of families by stressing the combination of education, training, and intensive case management. See Appendix B Item 6 for outcomes of our case management). Such families often have the potential for gainful employment, but because of a combination of complex reasons like the lack of transportation, and poor crisis management skills for example, they don't stay long in the job market or cannot gain the confidence to secure initial employment. What can be appreciated is that WRLP has put various organizational systems into place to accomplish its goals and make the program successful. It is through the efforts of businesses, staff, and other partners that this is made possible.

The three of the Annex staff where our education and social services are housed are University Trained Social Workers. Ms. Mary Reaves administered a Head Start Program for 18 years and directed the longest running faith based welfare-to-work mentoring program, Project Independence, which began in 1984 out of Greensboro Urban Ministry. Ms. Kristi Brooks and Minister Nancy McLean are degreed social workers. Minister McLean brings to the operation two years of social work experience she worked in Mt Zion's emergency assistance program. Ms. Traci Poole has a Bachelor's degree in business. The staff can relate to the participant and their families and collaborates with agencies to provide the services needed.

Reverend Cleveland, has a Masters Degree in Divinity, a BA in Business and was a trucking and distribution professional for 15 years. We use the Stephen R. Covey's *The Seven Habits of Highly Effective People*, as one of the texts in the training. Reverend Cleveland is a graduate of the Covey Leadership Training and a certified trainer.   Mr. Jeff Black, our operations manager at the distribution center has 19 years of business experience mainly in distribution, plus a BS degree in business and computer science. Ms Earlene Thomas, our job developer and job coach has two years of college and 15 years of business experience.

Partnerships

As a comprehensive community service agency we have worked with almost 200 agencies and churches (See Appendix Al Item 8-1, 8-2 for complete list). Some of the more recognizable names include: Gifts In-Kind International, United Way of Greater Greensboro, which has been our partner with Gifts In Kind International, Mt Zion Baptist Church, Starmount Presbyterian Church, Guilford Technical Community College who is our partner in human resource, instruction and computer training. NC A&T State University and UNC Greensboro have helped us both with technical assistance and they provide student interns. Guilford County Department Social Services is one of our strongest partners. Our partnership ranges from collaborative trainings to teaming up in planning the Faith Summit and numerous other joint activities. Alcohol and Drug Services helps us with individual client referral and services, and United Parcel Service has given us technical assistance and provided employment for our graduates.

The Weaver Foundation sees us as "social venture capital" and has become more than a funding partner. It is a major stakeholder in the larger community and sees us as the way to move people into stable careers, stable families, and stable neighborhoods by building people and institutions. We have numerous other relationships with a range of public and private agencies, churches and self help groups that we partner with to ensure effectiveness through our case management system with the students who are going from welfare to work.

Part III Demonstrated Effectiveness

Success in moving people from welfare to career paths involves the integration of job training, job development, job placement, and job retention. As of August of this past year we had 81% of our 100 (this does not include Class 7) graduates placed in full time employment averaging about $9.00 per hour. The recession has slowed our placement efforts but our workshop and coop have enabled us to weather the recession so far (See Appendix B Item 7-1,7-2 For August 2001 statistics). *Five of our graduates are now homeowners.* When we initially started three years ago, over a third of our students came to us with various health concerns that kept them form getting to class or training. As a result of partnering with the Moses Cone/Wesley Long Health Foundation we obtained the services of a Health Educator who helped us cut the health concerns in half.

We have addressed other barriers like inadequate transportation and poor housing through case management efforts. We reduced transportation problems by 50% and housing problems by 52%. The job retention aspect runs through every step of our program from the initial interview to having our graduates come back and help newcomers. The most important change is that people are getting careers, modeling for their children and striving for success. We are firm but gentle in our approach and as such we are seen in the community as a viable training center. While our program is voluntary, we have a waiting list of over 80 people.

Here are our recent awards: **2001 Nonprofit Sector Steward Award**, awarded to Welfare Reform Liaison Project, Inc., from N.C. Center for Nonprofits. **2000 "2 Those Who Care Award**," awarded to Rev. Cleveland from WFMY. **2000 Pinnacle Award,** awarded to Gifts in Kind Program from Gifts in Kind International. **2000 U.S. Department of Housing and Urban Development Regional Award,** awarded to Welfare Reform Liaison Project, Inc., and United Way of Greater Greensboro for the Welfare Reform Liaison Project, Inc. **2000 Outstanding Partnership Award,** awarded to Welfare Reform Liaison Project, Inc., from the N.C. Governor's Office. **1999 U.S. Department of Housing and Urban Development National Award,** awarded to Welfare Reform Liaison Project, Inc., and United Way of Greater Greensboro for the Welfare Reform Liaison Project, Inc. (See Appendix B Item 8-1, 8-2 for the news stories and letters).

Part IV Transition Plan.

Our current bylaws permit up to 20 positions but we currently have 15 members. One of those is representative of the poor.   Fourteen represent the business industry and other interests. To make the transition, we will expand our board to 42 members. We plan to add 13 more members from the low-income community through advertisements, word of mouth and public service announcements from our student base, housing projects, and/or some of the congregations that we partner with in the low-income community. That will give us 14 members representing the population we serve. We will add 14 elected officials or their designees giving us the balance required (See Appendix Al Items 9 and 10 and for list of elected officials and transition chart). We will have a board meeting to change the bylaws to make the transition legal. The opportunity excites us, if selected we look forward to hearing the needs and visions of the community. With the community's commitment and support lives can be changed.

CERTIFICATIONS AND ASSURANCES

CERTIFICATION OF ELIGIBILITY DOCUMENTS
The following documents are attached and reflect the current
status of the agency:

	YES	NO
1. Articles of Incorporation	X	
2. Most recent Audit or Schedule of Grantee Receipts and Expenditures Report	X	
3. Fidelity Bond	X	
4. Agency Bylaws	X	
5. Agency Personnel Policies and Procedures	X	
6. Manual Agency Financial Policies and Procedures Manual	X	
7. IRS 501(c)(3) Designation Letter	X	
8. Agency Organizational Chart	X	
9. Non-Discrimination Policy	X	
10. Indirect Cost Rate Agreement		X
11. Cost Allocation Plan	X	
12. Job Descriptions and Resumes of Executive Director and Finance Officer	X	

BOARD POWERS AND COMPOSITION
The Board of Directors has, at a minimum, the power to:

(If no, attach an explanation.)	YES	NO
1. Appoint Executive Director	X	
2. Determine personnel, organization, fiscal and program policies	X	
3. Determine overall program plans and priorities		
4. Make final approval of all programs, proposals and budgets	X	
5. Enforce compliance with all grant conditions	X	
6. Ensure the extent and quality of participation of the poor in the planning and evaluation of programs	X	

Are any of the above powers subject to concurrence, veto, or modification
by any other local official or authority, other than by delegation by the
governing board? (If yes, explain in the space provided below)

Are any of the above powers delegated?
(If yes, explain in the space provided below)   X

BOARD MEMBERSHIP

Total number of Board of Directors seats per bylaws: 20

MEMBERS OF THE BOARD OF DIRECTORS

Name   Address

Please see attached sheet.

Welfare Reform Liaison Project, Inc.
Board of Directors

Executive Committee

Ms. Lou Sua
1611 Valleywood Place
High Point, North Carolina 27265
(336) 841-5543
President

Mr. Marty Golds
Traffic & Warehouse Manager
Mother Murphy Laboratory
1855 Andrews Farm Road
Whitsett, North Carolina 27377
(336) 274-1637
Secretary

Mr. Robert Hamilton
Director of Pastoral Services The Moses Cone
Health System
1200 N. Elm Street
Greensboro, North Carolina 27401-1020
(336) 832-7950
Vice-President

Mr. Ruf'us Stanley
Public Health Inspector
Infectious Disease Division
Guilford County Health Department
2216 Lakeland Road
Greensboro, North Carolina 27406
(336) 373-3184
Treasurer

Board Members

Pastor George Brooks
Senior Pastor
Mt. Zion Baptist Church
1301 Alamance Church Road
Greensboro, North Carolina 27406
(336) 273-7930

Mr. William Buster
Mary Reynolds Babcock Foundation
2522 Reynolds Road
Winston-Salem, North Carolina 27106
(336) 748-9222

Captain Julian Davis
Police Captain City of Greensboro
12 Oliver Court
Greensboro, North Carolina 27406
(336)412-5753

Ms. Robin Lee
Customer Service Team Leader
Pitney Bowes Management
3907 Standish Drive
Greensboro, North Carolina 27401
(336) 805-3383

Mr. Kevin Bumgarner
Editor
The Business Journal
100 S. Main St, Suite 400
Greensboro, North Carolina 27401
(336) 271-6539

Ms. Bertha Carter
Director of Recruitment &
Selection American Express
7701 Airport Center Drive
Greensboro, North Carolina 27409-9047
(336) 668-5954

Ms. Elizabeth James
Manager
Public Transportation Division Greensboro
Department of Transportation
1689 Youngs Mill Road
Greensboro, North Carolina 27406
(336) 373-2820

Mr. M. Lee McAllister
President/CEO
Weaver Investment Company
324 W. Wendover Avenue
Greensboro, North Carolina 27408
(336) 275-9600

THIS IS TO CERTIFY THAT TO THE BEST OF MY KNOWLEDGE, THE INFORMATION CONTAINED IN THIS APPLICATION IS CORRECT AND RECEIVED APPROVAL FOR SUBMISSION BY THE BOARD OF DIRECTORS.

Signature of Board Chairperson
Lou Sua

Typed Name of Board Chairperson

Welfare Reform Liaison Project, Inc.
Agency

January 17, 2002
Date

APPENDIX 7

Faith Summit 2009—Events of the Day and Sponsors

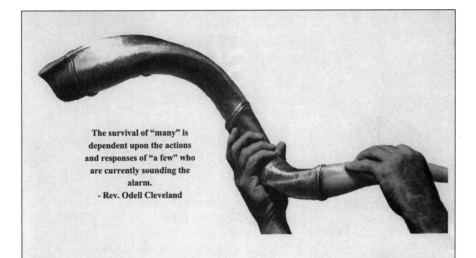

The survival of "many" is dependent upon the actions and responses of "a few" who are currently sounding the alarm.
- Rev. Odell Cleveland

Welfare Reform **LIAISON** Project, Inc. O.I.C. C.A.A.

Welfare Reform Liaison Project Mission Statement

It shall be the mission of Welfare Reform Liaison Project, Inc. to provide services that enable economically disadvantaged individuals and families to move toward self-sufficiency through collaboration with federal and state agencies, the faith community, corporations, other agencies from both the public and private sector, as well as the local citizenry.

2009 Guilford County Community Faith Summit
Sponsored by Welfare Reform Liaison Project, Inc., O.I.C. - C.A.A.
Hosted by Mt. Zion Baptist Church of Greensboro, Inc.
1301 Alamance Church Rd., Greensboro, N.C.

Lessons Learned:
"Past, Present and Future"

Building a Community on a Foundation of
"Common Ground"

~ Thursday, May 7, 2009 ~

TIME	EVENT
7:45 a.m. – 8:45 a.m.	Pre-Registration, On-Site Registration, **Continental Breakfast**
8:45 a.m. – 10:00 a.m.	**Opening Session**

Welcome Remarks..Reverend Odell Cleveland.
President & CEO, Welfare Reform Liaison Project, Inc., O.I.C. - C.A.A.

Greeting

United States Senator Kay Hagan..Melissa Midgett
North Carolina Director

U. S. Congressional District 6...Lindsay Morris
Community Liaison, Office of Congressman Howard Coble, NC-6

U. S. Congressional District 13....................................Ronald D. Williams, II
District Liaison, Office of Congressman Brad Miller, NC-13

North Carolina House of Representatives, District 60...........................Earl Jones
Chair, Guilford County Legislative Delegations

Guilford County Commissioner....................................Melvin "Skip" Alston
Chair, Guilford County Board of Commissioners

City of Greensboro..Mayor Yvonne Johnson

City of High Point...TBA

Welfare Reform Liaison Project, Inc., O.I.C.-C.A.A.,.......................Bernita Sims
WRLP Board Chair
High Point City Council, Ward One

Invocation ....Dr. Sid Batts
First Presbyterian Church

Tribute Presentation of Shofar Award .....Reverend Odell Cleveland and Bernita Sims

Special Announcements...Ron Surgeon
Welfare Reform Liaison Project, Inc., O.I.C.-C.A.A., Board Member

TIME	WORKSHOPS

10:15 a.m. – 11:30 a.m.

First Lesson Learned:

National Community Service
Facilitators: *Wes Ward and Ron Brooks*
This session will be a discussion of how reinvesting into our community will allow us to connect to common ground issues and challenges which will lead to a stronger foundation. National Community Service connects individuals (in all stages of their life) to service opportunities that allow them to give their time in different ways such as: AmeriCorps, AmeriCorps*VISTA and RSVP.
Presenters: *Betty Platt, N.C. State Office Senior Program Director, Corporation for National & Community Services; Alicia Hartsfield, Senior AmeriCorps Program Officer, N.C. Commission on Volunteerism and Community Service; and Shelly Sitko, RSVP Director, Senior Resources of Guilford*

Second Lesson Learned:

Housing Options Today
Facilitator: *T. Dianne Bellamy-Small*
This session will focus on the "reality" of what some of our community members are facing during this economic struggle; There will also be an update of the plans, alternatives, avenues and solutions that are available to circumvent the worst scenario.
Presenters: *Tami Hinton, Director of Consumer Affairs, Office of the Commissioner of Banks; Richard Lee, Foreclosure Prevention Team Leader, North Carolina Housing Finance Agency; K. Jehan Benton, Director, Partners Ending Homelessness, Family Service of the Piedmont; and M. Lynn Jarvis, Esq., Foreclosure Prevention Fellow, Office of the Commissioner of Banks*

Third Lesson Learned:

The Community of Faith: The Role of Faith-Based Organizations in System of Care
Facilitators: *Earnest Miller and Darryl Jones*
Participants will be asked to assist in developing the next steps related to forming collaborations among congregations, community service agencies and community leaders. Workshop leaders will share recently gathered information from 80 representatives of these groups and an example of a current program that addresses services available to those in need. Participants will brainstorm opportunities to move forward to maximize services throughout the community and how to offer those services to those who need them most.
Presenters: *Bob Wineburg Ph. D., Jefferson Pilot Excellence Professor, School of Human Environmental Sciences, Department of Social Work, UNC Greensboro; Jean H. Davison, Vice Chairperson, Kleemeir Christian Ethics Forum of the First Presbyterian Church; and Keith Barsuhn, President and Chief Executive Officer, United Way of Greater Greensboro*

Fourth Lesson Learned:

Latino Entrepreneurialism
Facilitator: *Ron Surgeon*
The American Dream refers to the freedom that allows all citizens and all residents of the United States to pursue their goals in life through hard work and free choice. The American Dream often refers to the opportunity for immigrants to achieve greater material prosperity than was possible in their countries of origin. This session will focus on new and exciting efforts to develop and encourage business development within a rapidly growing community.
Presenters: *Dr. H. Nolo Martinez, Welfare Reform Liaison Project., Inc., Latino Pathways Adviser; Victor Dau, Director Small Business Center, Randolph Community College; and Armando Soto, Latino Business Owner, 2 Businesses in the Triad*

Fifth Lesson Learned:

Making Good Health Happen: The Guilford Community Care Network: Assuring Healthcare for All
Facilitators: *Karen Martinez and Jackie Lucas*
This session will focus on how the Guilford Community Care Network addresses uninsured patients, health care costs and access to medical care for those who are at or below 225% of the federal poverty level. This session will share state level findings to this innovative approach. The GCCN represents the integrated medical home model that focuses on a coordinated system of care with shared resources and information; standardized eligibility and enrollment and case management. The Network is centered on patient care and access to care.
Presenters: *Lisa Duck, Project Manager for the Guilford Community Care Network; Brian Ellerby, Executive Director, Guilford Adult Health, Inc. and Guilford Child Health, Inc.; Anne Braswell, Senior Analyst and HealthNet Program Manager, N.C. Department of Health and Human Services; Claudette Johnson, President, Partnership for Health Management; and Shaunesi Griffin, Program Manager, Partnership for Health Management's Uninsured Program*

Sixth Lesson Learned:

How to Survive the Economy: Facing a Bad Economy with Good Faith
Facilitator: *Bernita Sims*
A forum to explore ways in which we can work together and build alliances that will allow us to more effectively deal with community problems as we go forward as a Faith Community. The focus will be on programs that assist the unemployed; address their situation.
Presenters: *Mark Brainerd, Associate Pastor, Congregational Care & Outreach Ministries, Westminster Presbyterian Church; David Moff, CEO, The H R Group, Inc.; Betsy Gamburg, Director of Jewish Family Services; Lisa Cozart, Quick Jobs Program Assistant, Guilford Technical Community College and Vivek Kshetrapal, Career Development, Job Link Career Center.*

Seventh Lesson Learned:

Resource Development: Moving Beyond the Grant
Facilitator: *Elder Cliff Lovick*
This session workshop will focus on strategies for funding community serving efforts with revenues other than government or foundation grants. Successful examples of non-grant revenue development by some of the country's most innovative non-profits will be highlighted. Lastly, "worst practices" of non-profit attempts at forming business ventures will also be discussed.
Presenters: *Billy Terry, Business Operations Officer, Office of the Chief Administrative Officer, Washington Metropolitan Transit Authority; and Reverend Odell Cleveland, President & CEO, Welfare Reform Liaison Project, Inc., O.I.C.-C.A.A.*

Eighth Lesson Learned:	*Connecting with Guilford County Schools* **Facilitator:** *Faye Stanley and Cheryl Hairston* Have you ever wanted to volunteer at a Guilford County School (GCS) but wasn't sure where to start? Would your faith community or non-profit organization like to adopt a school or partner with the school district? Find out about the district's new strategic plan, and how that plan ties into volunteer recruitment, student mentoring and business/community partnerships. Learn about student, school and district needs, and find out how to connect with Guilford County Schools. Come away with a toolkit for getting started in GCS as a volunteer or community partner. **Presenters:** *Nora Carr, Chief of Staff, Guilford County Schools; and Cecilia Adams, Community Relations Manager, Guilford County Schools*
11:30 a.m. – 12:10 p.m.	Break / Time Allotted For Everyone To Go To <u>Lower Level</u> To Pick Up Their Boxed Lunches and Enjoy Their Meal
12:10 p.m. – 1:15 p.m.	Introduction of the Speakers...Richard "Skip" Moore *President, The Weaver Foundation*
	Keynote Speakers
	Melissa Rogers, *serves on President Barack Obama's Advisory Council on Faith-Based and Neighborhood Partnership; Director of Wake Forest University Divinity School's Center for Religion and Public Affairs*
	Keith Barsuhn, *President and CEO, United Way of Greater Greensboro*
	Bernita Sims, *Board Chair, Welfare Reform Liaison Project, Inc., O.I.C.-C.A.A. City of High Point Council Member*
1:15 p.m. – 1:30 p.m.	Break

1:30 p.m. – 3:00 p.m.   *Sessions I – III*

Session I

Located in the Fellowship Hall

Interfaith Clergy Trip to Israel (In Partnership with the Community Foundation of Greater Greensboro)
Facilitator: *Reverend Odell Cleveland*
This session will consist of a video and discussion focusing on the trip's impact on the community. The trip served as a way to greatly strengthen the social capital found within the faith community.
Presenter: *Reverend Sid Batts, First Presbyterian Church; Rabbi Fred Guttman, Temple Emanuel; Reverend Richard Johnson, We are One Christian Fellowship; Reverend Diane Givens Moffet, St. James Presbyterian Church; and Reverend Adrian Starks, Anderson Grove Baptist Church*

Session II
Located in the Chapel

The New Struggle: From Civil Rights to Silver Rights
Facilitator: Faye Stanley
This forum will bring together community leaders to explore the potential economic impact of the opening of the International Civil Rights Center & Museum on the Greensboro community and the Triad region. Cultural tourism is the fastest growing segment of this industry and the museum will bring both economic and quality of life assets to those who live, work and visit our growing and vibrant downtown area. Business leaders and those who work in collaboration with the hospitality industry will share their feedback regarding how the Museum raises the profile of the city for prospective corporations and individual clients seeking sites for relocation in addition to support for public and private educational institutions across the state and nation.
Presenters: *Melvin "Skip" Alston, Chariman, Guilford County Board of Commissioners; Chairman, International Civil Rights Center and Museum; Earl Jones, North Carolina House of Representatives, Vice Chairman, International Civil Rights Center & Museum; Richard "Skip" Moore, President, The Weaver Foundation; Gail Murphy, Director of Marketing, Greensboro Convention and Visitors Bureau; April Harris, Executive Director, Action Greensboro; and Amelia Parker, Executive Director, International Civil Rights Center & Museum*

Session III
Located in the Library

Education Matters….. What difference can you make?
Facilitator: *Amos Quick*
Supporting Education must be the number one priority of Gilford County so that we have high quality schools and our students are prepared for the 21ˢᵗ Century global workforce! This session will be a presentation with data and information on how residents of Guilford County Schools….compares to other urban districts in North Carolina and information on how residents of Guilford County are supporting education, with ideas on ways you can be involved. The Teacher Supply Warehouse, DonorsChoose.org, and advocacy! Discussion and lots of ideas! Come ready to share and discuss
Presenter: *Margaret Arbuckle, Executive Director, Guilford Education Alliance*

The Welfare Reform Liaison Project Inc., Shofar Award is presented to organizations and individuals who have provided support to WRLP over the course of many years and in many different ways. The Shofar is usually made from a ram's horn. It was used by the ancient Hebrews in battle, during religious ceremonies, and as a call to assembly.

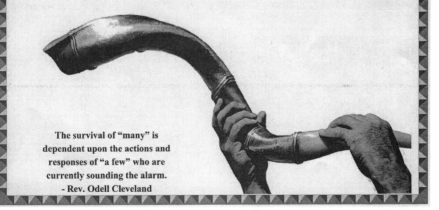

The survival of "many" is dependent upon the actions and responses of "a few" who are currently sounding the alarm.
- Rev. Odell Cleveland

Welfare Reform Liaison Project, O.I.C. - C.A.A. wish to thank all of our partners for assisting in making this event possible.

THE GREENSBORO TIMES

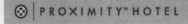

United Way of Greater Greensboro

United Way of High Point

INDEX

ABOUT THE AUTHORS

The Reverend Odell Cleveland (BS, *University of South Carolina* at Spartanburg; MDiv, Hood Theological Seminary) is the president/CEO and cofounder of the Welfare Reform Liaison Project, Inc. (WRLP) in Greensboro, North Carolina. He is a graduate of a number of leadership programs, including Harvard Divinity School's Summer Leadership Institute. He has served as adjunct professor for Duke University's certificate program in nonprofit management, as instructor in North Carolina A&T State University's Minority Enterprise Training and Development Program, and as instructor in the department of social work at the University of North Carolina, Greensboro. He is also a nationally certified peer-to-peer trainer in Results Oriented Management and Accountability (ROMA).

The Reverend Cleveland has extensive professional and volunteer experience ranging from board leadership roles to city government work. He has served in board leadership capacities for agencies such as Joseph's House and Malachi House. He serves as a member of the Action Greensboro II Core Committee, as well as the United Way of Greater Greensboro's Thriving at Three Initiative Committee. He is currently active as chair of the Quick Jobs Advisory Committee for Guilford Technical Community College and serves on the Finance Committee and Board of Directors of the United Way of Greater Greensboro.

Professor Robert Wineburg (MSW, *Syracuse University*; PhD, *University of Pittsburgh*) is the Jefferson Pilot Excellence Professor of Social Work at the University of North Carolina, Greensboro. In 2010, he was appointed as director of community-engaged scholarship for the School of Human Environmental Sciences at UNC Greensboro. In 2007, his former students fully endowed the Bob Wineburg Scholarship in Community Services, making him the only active faculty member at his university with a completely student-funded scholarship in his name.

His work with his congregational research partner, Professor Ram Cnaan of the University of Pennsylvania, simultaneously and independently examined the partnerships between agencies and religious congregations and the social services provided by congregations themselves (see faithsurvey.uwde.org for more information). Professor Wineburg has authored or coauthored three books and more than 75 papers and articles. He has worked locally and nationally with many agencies and organizations, including, from its inception, the Welfare Reform Liaison Project.